Remembering
the Master

Other books by Sid Campbell
and Greglon Yimm Lee

The Dragon and the Tiger: The Birth of Bruce Lee's Jeet Kune Do, The Oakland Years: Volume 1

The Dragon and the Tiger: The Untold Story of Jun Fan Gung-fu and James Yimm Lee, The Oakland Years: Volume 2

Remembering the Master

Bruce Lee, James Yimm Lee,
and the Creation of Jeet Kune Do

Sid Campbell
and Greglon Yimm Lee

BLUE SNAKE BOOKS

Berkeley, California

Published by Blue Snake Books / Frog, Ltd.

Blue Snake Books / Frog, Ltd. books are distributed by North Atlantic Books
P.O. Box 12327
Berkeley, California 94712

Cover and text design by Brad Greene
Printed in the United States of America
Distributed to the book trade by
Publishers Group West

Blue Snake Books' publications are available through most bookstores. For further information, call 800-337-2665 or visit our website at www.northatlanticbooks.com or www.bluesnakebooks.com.

Substantial discounts on bulk quantities are available to corporations, professional associations, and other organizations. For details and discount information, contact our special sales department.

PLEASE NOTE: The creators and publishers of this book disclaim any liabilities for loss in connection with following any of the practices, exercises, and advice contained herein. To reduce the chance of injury or any other harm, the reader should consult a professional before undertaking this or any other martial arts, movement, meditative arts, health, or exercise program. The instructions and advice printed in this book are in not any way intended as a substitute for medical, mental, or emotional counseling with a licensed physician or healthcare provider.

Library of Congress Cataloging-in-Publication Data

Lee, Greglon, 1953–
    Remembering the master : Bruce Lee, James Yimm Lee, and the creation of Jeet Kune Do / by Greglon Yimm Lee and Sid Campbell.
        p. cm.
    Summary: "Remembering the Master is a glimpse into the lives of Bruce Lee and James Yimm Lee, related through the memories of those closest to them during the Oakland years, where they changed the course of martial arts history with the creation of Jeet Kune Do"—Provided by publisher.
    ISBN 1-58394-148-7 (trade paper)
    1. Lee, Bruce, 1940–1973. 2. Lee, J. Yimm (James Yimm) 3. Martial artists—United States—Biography. 4. Jeet Kune Do. I. Campbell, Sid. II. Title.
    GV1113.A2L444 2006
    791.43028'092—dc22
                                                    2006033989
                                                    CIP

1 2 3 4 5 6 7 8 9 DATA 12 11 10 09 08 07 06

Dedication

This special memoriam edition, *Remembering the Master: Bruce Lee, James Yimm Lee, and the Creation of Jeet Kune Do,* is dedicated to all of the students, families, and friends of Bruce Lee and James Yimm Lee who contributed to this work. Your kindness, graciousness, and willingness to share are so deeply appreciated. Otherwise, this edition would have never been possible to archive for the sake of posterity and biographical history.

We are eternally humbled.

Sid Campbell

Greglon Yimm Lee

Contents

Foreword

A Place in History

Like a comet streaking across the clear evening sky, Bruce radiated a powerful aura and left behind a torrent of immense energy in his wake. He literally captivated everyone's attention who witnessed his phenomenal brilliance. After all, he was Bruce Lee.

It is understood that Bruce Lee has become a 20th-century icon. His short, yet illuminating, life on this earth has left an indelible impression that will undoubtedly be felt by millions more for many generations to come.

He was a man with an undaunted vision, driven by perfection and striving to reach incredible plateaus that challenged him at every turn of his young life. The seeds of this vision were first planted and truly began to take form after he and his wife Linda Emery Lee relocated from Seattle, Washington, to Oakland, California.

During their initial meeting, and before relocating to Oakland, he and James Lee had numerous discussions revolving around the subject of martial arts. We believe this to be the point in time when Bruce began anew by formulating bigger plans that he was certain would produce more favorable results than any of his previous endeavors.

It was in essence the end of one chapter of Bruce's life. Up until the time he and Linda took up residency at the home of the James Yimm Lee family at 3039 Monticello Avenue, his life had been loosely orchestrated around small dreams and temporary plans that oftentimes produced minuscule results. The Oakland Years were a new beginning.

Though the scenery had changed, and the situational circumstances were different, James' accommodating guidance, advice, and collaborative assistance seemed to alleviate some of the financial burdens and temporarily change the dynamics of his and Linda's uncertain future. However, as in Seattle, there were again many times during their residency in Oakland that there seemed to be more questions than answers as to how he and Linda would overcome the perplexingly insurmountable hurdles that lay ahead of them. During this time of uncertainty, there was one certainty: this was the turning point in time and perhaps the primary factor that drastically changed the way Bruce Lee perceived his destiny.

One would think that the Oakland Years were a necessary period that the young, newly married Bruce Lee needed in order to reassess his life and start embracing Linda's priorities for establishing a family. And definitely a time for him to begin taking responsibility for his actions. James Lee's support and sage-like, oftentimes visionary advice undoubtedly factored into the scenario of Bruce Lee becoming so strongly focused on the goals that would ultimately become his destiny and earn him a place in the annals of history.

James continually encouraged Bruce that the martial arts, and numerous opportunities that could arise from it, were somewhere out there in the future, for someone who had his natural athletic talents, keen sense of wit, intelligent rationale, and personal integrity and could put it to use. Bruce Lee needed to hear this from someone he respected and trusted...and that someone was James Yimm Lee.

In hindsight, as simple as James' advice seemed at the time, the Oakland Years were still a time when Bruce Lee—or anyone else, for that matter, who wanted to earn a substantial income from the martial arts—was going to have to wait until the American public was ready to embrace the cultural ethos embodying the Asian fighting arts. James spoke from experience because he had already been down those roads before and knew that as easy as it seemed, it would take a lot of hard work and perseverance, and one who embarked on such a venture would have to wait until the world was ready to accept this type of business venture into their society. Bruce's grand plan—opening a select chain of Jun Fan Gung Fu Institutes, earning additional income from published books, using his teaching talents as a cha-cha teacher, becoming independent enough to call his own shots, raising a family—all were real possibilities for future consideration but did little to solve his immediate needs for financial security. Here he and Linda were relying on the graciousness of close friends to sustain themselves as Bruce struggled to formulate a practical business plan for the future.

Bruce Lee finally realized that to achieve success and unleash the greatness within himself, he had to draw from every resource at his disposal. He reinvented himself many times, at many levels, to accomplish what he did in his short life. Through hard work, determination, diligence, and using his resourcefulness, he struggled to accomplish everything that he attempted.

After reading a rough draft of *The Dragon and the Tiger: The Birth of Bruce Lee's Jeet Kune Do in Oakland* during the weekend she was attending Bruce's Walk of Fame dedication ceremony in Hollywood, Linda Lee shared with co-author Greglon Yimm Lee, "I had forgotten just how hard of a struggle Bruce and I had during those early years. But, we never gave up. Those were trying times that strengthened us both for the things that lay ahead. Your father James was our salvation at the time. And you and Karena were a special joy in our lives."

Yes, the Oakland Years were very trying times for Linda and Bruce Lee. But they accomplished some amazing and astounding results. In fact, most people—even those with very fertile imaginations— would find it difficult to fathom the difficulties that this couple encountered. And James Lee was there for them all along their journey through this uncertain time.

The fusion of energy between Bruce Lee and James Yimm Lee was the catalyst, and perhaps in part was responsible, for endowing Bruce with the tools and wherewithal to confront these challenges that would lay ahead. After James' wife Katherine's demise from complications arising from breast cancer, Linda, Bruce, and James' cohesion grew even stronger. For what had originally been perceived as a mere symbiotic relationship soon evolved into one of real love and compassion for each other. It is obvious from the chronicles in Volumes 1 and 2 of *The Dragon and the Tiger* that they formed a bond of closeness that would last all the days of Bruce Lee's life. That bond is still shared today by Linda and her godchildren Karena Beverly and Greglon, who still reside in the San Francisco Bay Area.

Although it is not widely known by the millions of people who have been influenced by her husband Bruce Lee, Linda was a very strong influence in his life. For that, she has never really been recognized for her contribution and moral support during those most crucial Oakland Years. Most are not even aware of her unceasing devotion to raising Karena Beverly Lee and Greglon Yimm Lee during their formative years. She was the maternal figure and played a vital role of taking care of the children, cloistering them from the fears and uncertainties of a life without their mother, and at the same time balanced her time nurturing support for Bruce's dreams to be successful. This, while helping James Yimm Lee cope with the hardships of the emotional stress of those bleak times immediately after Katherine's death and when he was at the lowest point in his life. She was their fortress in the storm of life. She was enduring. She was strong. She was compassionate. And, above all, she provided much-needed support by sharing her unmitigated love with the children and the men in her life.

Those fond memories still linger as a testament to her importance during that crucial time in the children's life. When Brandon Bruce Lee was born in Oakland, Linda assumed yet another role. She became a mother in her own right.

We feel that these words need to be expressed in this foreword to *Remembering the Master: Bruce Lee, James Yimm Lee, and the Creation of Jeet Kune Do*. Bruce, Linda, and Brandon left some very vivid memories reflecting the happiness they brought to the family, students, and friends who shared in their lives during those uncertain times.

As you begin perusing this memoriam edition, please take the time to reflect on those early times before the world knew who Bruce Lee and James Yimm Lee were . . . and the course they were charting that would change martial arts as the world knows it today. The third piece of Bruce Lee's much documented life that has been previously unchronicled, this "In Memoriam" edition honors the memory of Bruce and James in a way that we believe is a befitting memorial to these "Warriors of the Way."

We have also tried very hard to capture the pure essence of these two exceptional martial artists at a time when they were developing their fighting concepts of jeet kune do, or The Way of the Intercepting Fist, which would later become known to the world as simply JKD.

The collaborative efforts of Bruce and James through exhaustive postulations, theoretical trial and error, and experimentation produced a serious new way of looking at practical self-defense from the perspective of reality. In their quest for a new truth, they discovered themselves, their art, and the simplicity of life. It was in a basement garage on Monticello Avenue in Oakland, California, where these historical findings were developed that the world now practices.

Humbly,
The Authors

Introduction

Under the category of "Heroes & Icons," Bruce Lee has been chosen by *Time* magazine as one of the 100 Most Influential People in the 20th Century. This prestigious accolade places him among such historical luminaries as Muhammad Ali, Charles Lindbergh, Marilyn Monroe, the Kennedys, and the Beatles.

"Bruce Lee was ahead of his time by at least a hundred years!" At a time when the terms "karate" and "gung-fu" were synonymous with the mystical Oriental fighting arts shrouded in deep secrecy and taught only to immediate members of the families bearing their Asian heritages, Bruce Lee was streaking across the western sky like a giant meteor, bringing to the world his unique philosophy and martial arts acumen.

Indeed, Bruce Lee did leave behind a legacy that is still being felt more than thirty years past his premature death on July 20, 1973. In the relatively short period since his birth in San Francisco, California, entering the world in the Year of the Dragon, nobody expected Bruce Lee to become one of the greatest and most enduring martial artists and Asian-American movie stars the world has ever known.

His influence has been felt by millions around the world and presumably will have a profound effect on countless millions a hundred years from now. Nevertheless, several questions still remain.

"Who had a profound influence on Bruce Lee's life?" "Who were his friends and confidants?" and "What inspirations and ideologies did Bruce Lee draw from to postulate his way of life that would become known to the world's masses as jeet kune do, The Way of the Intercepting Fist?"

Clearly, in the decades since his demise, and as an attempt to record the effects of his illumination, there have been millions of words and thousands of stories, documentaries, biographical and literary historical works, and oftentimes entertaining accounts of his life during the 20th century.

In a manner of speaking, our multi-volume work titled *The Dragon and the Tiger*, which has spanned a period of twenty years of diligent and unrelenting research, is an attempt to explore and answer these unresolved questions.

To discover the reasons behind his phenomenal rise to fame as one of the most influential human beings in the 20th century requires exploring far beyond the media hype and sensationalism that has largely superficially exploited and exaggerated disproportionately who Bruce Lee was as a man.

We set about to learn more about who Bruce Lee was from an entirely different perspective from that of media sensationalism or literary accounts written by those who did not know him personally. What better way to discover who a person is than through family and close friends with whom Bruce Lee spent his formative years before his luminary rise to superstardom.

Greglon Yimm Lee's father was truly one of the men in Bruce Lee's life whom he respected and trusted like very few in his life—legendary gung-fu pioneer James Yimm Lee, a gung-fu teacher, bodybuilder, publisher, freethinker, martial arts author, inventor, and philosopher in his own right and a man whom Bruce Lee shared much with over the years they spent together in Oakland, California.

It was a time when Bruce and his wife Linda Emery Lee lived with James Yimm Lee and his family during those turbulent times we fondly recall as "the Oakland Years."

It was there that Bruce Lee truly began to find himself and realize his potential as a martial artist, as a man with a purpose in life, and as a family man where he and Linda proudly became parents with the birth of Brandon Lee. It was also there that he and James Yimm Lee became more than friends. They became comrades-in-arms, confidants, and business partners and shared much of their martial arts knowledge for their mutual benefit. It was essentially their collaboration together during the Oakland Years that formed the basis of the concepts that would become known to the world simply as "jeet kune do."

During the Oakland Years Bruce Lee met many new friends who would become students under both his and James Lee's gung-fu tutelage. This book is an effort to capture the memories, recollections, and reflections of their friends and students and hopefully provide another glimpse into the lives of these great men and the influence that was left behind after their premature demises.

Remembering the Master: Bruce Lee, James Yimm Lee, and the Creation of Jeet Kune Do is an assemblage of letters that were written by family, students, and loved ones who respected both men immensely. Most of these treasured missives were penned twenty years ago when *The Dragon and the Tiger: The Birth of Bruce Lee's Jeet Kune Do* series was first being researched. These letters chronicle the times when Bruce was beginning his rise from anonymity to stardom of the likes that no man in the martial arts had ever achieved before. These were times when the history of the martial arts in the United States was just beginning. These were times when Bruce Lee's fame was shared with only a few trusted friends and students who trained with him and James Yimm Lee in a small, unpretentious garage on Monticello Avenue in Oakland, California.

It is our sincere belief that if you truly want to discover the greatness behind influential personages who have had a profound impact on the world at large, it helps to see them from the perspective of their family and friends. That is what we have attempted to do with this biographical assemblage of historical letters and recollections.

We hope that the countless millions of martial artists who loved both Bruce Lee and James Yimm Lee will read and reminisce about the times when history was actually being made and the martial arts were on a path that would lead to prominence, thanks to the likes of Bruce Lee and James Yimm Lee.

The Authors
Sid Campbell
Greglon Yimm Lee

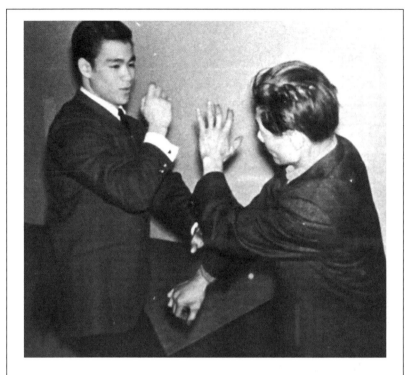

Part One

Part

One

A Tribute

During the course of researching the *The Dragon and the Tiger: The Birth of Bruce Lee's Jeet Kune Do in Oakland* book series, we interviewed many of Jimmy Lee's closest friends, students, and family members. Their gracious contributions and fond recollections made it possible to bring closure to this memoriam edition by creating a memorable and historically noteworthy tribute to honor James Yimm Lee. These close friends and students opened their hearts and shared in the recall of memories, anecdotes, stories, and experiences that had had such a profound impact on their own lives. Their recollections and contributed photographs from the time are intended to show and tell as much about James Yimm Lee that is humanly possible within this historical work. For these contributions, the authors are forever gratefully indebted.

Also, as we collected and chronicled the historical memorabilia herein, we strove to present a part of James to the world of martial arts that possibly may never have been revealed before.

He was indeed an extraordinary man, in that throughout his life he chose to refrain from immodesty and never really cared for public notoriety, although it was sometimes necessary in order to accomplish the objectives of publishing his various martial arts books.

Essentially, James Yimm Lee was quite content to stay out of the limelight and let others, including his close friend and confidant, Bruce Lee, enjoy the glory and receive the accolades for contributions that he helped make to the growth and development of martial arts in the United States.

His pupils, as illustrated and documented in this book, will provide you with a glimpse of the impact that he still has through the achievements of those who trained directly with him and/or Bruce Lee in the Bay Area during a time when the martial arts was not quite yet a household word. We think you'll agree that James Yimm Lee's presence will be felt for many generations to come.

Before the release of the historical archives through *The Dragon and the Tiger* series, few would have ever known him for his book-publishing talents, his vehement tenacity, his physical toughness, and his straightforward "no-holds-barred" approach to life. We can also say, with great candor, that Bruce Lee recognized this no-nonsense approach to life philosophy almost immediately after he met James for the first time.

Over the course of time, during the Oakland Years (1962–1965), Bruce Lee continually praised James for his creative genius, his martial arts prowess, and the many invaluable contributions he brought to the concepts behind the development of "jeet kune do."

Bruce Lee was certainly among James' closest friends, but their relation was also much more than that. They were like family in every sense of the word. In addition, they were mentors to each other at several levels and shared so much in common, with each teaching the other from his own personal experiences and from life in general. They were business partners, cohorts, comrades, brothers-in-arms, confidants, sounding boards, and to some extent "devil's advocates" when either had an idea that needed some input. They laughed together, they shared the anguish of losing loved ones, they basked in each other's successes, they helped each other accomplish their goals, and they were both innovators who were years ahead of their times.

As is so eloquently stated in one of our featured contributing letters, "They were struck from the same mold." And just for the record, it was his comrade Bruce Lee who stuck with James to the end during his last days on this earth. In fact, many do not know that although Bruce was in Hong Kong at the time, he continually called James in Oakland and wanted him to play a major role in his movie *The Chinese Connection*. But James had to decline because of failing health and instead suggested that Bruce feature their student Bob Baker from the Oakland JKD kwoon. Bruce solemnly honored that request. Today this decision is so indelibly etched in the annals of cinematic history with the late Bob Baker playing the villain in *The Chinese Connection*.

Bruce Lee was also the technical editor of James Yimm Lee's last published book, *Wing Chun Kung-fu*, produced by Ohara Publications. This is an interesting footnote in history when you stop to consider that James was the publisher of Bruce's very first book, *Chinese Gung-Fu: The Philosophical Art of Self-Defense*. For martial arts enthusiasts who have followed the lives and times of these men, they may see the *yin-yang* inference here.

Though James Lee never dwelled on the negative or catastrophic events that occurred in his life, he was a very sensitive, yet strong-willed individualist. Bruce and he were very similar in this regard as well. Both would take the bad or negative accounts in stride and move forward with renewed determination to use the experience to improve their conditions. It could be said that they both used obstacles as stepping-stones on their roads to accomplishing the things they did.

Aside from these given tangibles, few knew that James Lee nearly died of malaria during World War II, while participating in the military campaigns that raged in the Philippine Islands. His body was drastically weakened by this malady but his survival instinct and strong fighting spirit never wavered as he returned to America and became a patient for several months at the Veterans Hospital in San Francisco.

Few never really knew that the debilitating effects left by this traumatic experience were the primary reasons that he began serious bodybuilding in the first place. This was a decision that required months and months of hard work and discipline and would ultimately culminate with him entering competition and becoming a California state weightlifting champion. His fascination with the pugilistic arts also led him to excel, with artful proficiency, as an amateur boxer, and later he even earned a brown belt in judo before beginning training in *sil lum* gung-fu. It is also of interest that both Bruce and James were experienced amateur boxers and had many similar parallels in other ways as well.

Though he never chose to flaunt it, James had close friends who included world-renowned health and fitness guru Jack LaLanne, bodybuilding titleholder Jack Dillinger, and numerous boxers who hailed from the Oakland-San Francisco Bay Area. One, in particular, was junior welterweight contender Johnny Gonsalves. In Oakland, because of his kinship with all of the shop owners and patrons who frequented the Chinese district, James was affectionately known as "The Mayor of Chinatown."

Prior to Bruce Lee, James was one of the very first American-born Chinese in the United States and Western world to teach

Caucasians the art of gung-fu. And, according to many lifelong martial arts experts, he was the first person to use the word "kung-fu" to describe the Chinese forms of martial arts. Up until that time, pronunciation was "gung-fu" among Westernized martial artists, and "gong fu" by the ethnic Chinese who were skilled in these open-hand styles of self-defense. He did this to create visually appealing front covers for several of his books. It caught on and today is the commonly accepted way that the Chinese art of self-defense is known throughout the modern world.

Even among his martial arts peers, and including the rest of the world, many did not know, or were not aware, of James' other unique talents. It was simply not in his nature to brag or boast about his varied skills or accomplishments. However, James was a first-rate inventor who never chose to patent his designs. He developed many innovative pieces of martial arts training equipment for his own use and later for his training partner Bruce Lee.

As this "In Memoriam" volume will attest, James Yimm Lee was a man with many talents who had many friends who recognized his uniqueness. The contents of subsequent chapters will bear out why his relatives, close friends, and martial arts students thought so highly of him.

What is also fascinating is that Bruce Lee found James' subtle humor and straightforward approach to dealing with situations and life in general intellectually stimulating and quite provocative. As a Chinese-American with similar interests and commonalities, it was easy to see that in another like-minded individual. Bruce had a keen eye and was very perceptive of individuals who had similar qualities as himself. They were both critical as well as perfectionistic in everything they pursued. Perhaps that is why they were meant to meet each other and become partners in the first place.

After thoroughly contemplating the contents of this massive, pictorially illustrated memorial edition, you will perhaps draw the same conclusion that many who knew both James Lee and Bruce Lee did . . . that they were so similar in so many ways. They had a fighting spirit and a zest for life that was never sated, at least not until a project or an idea of some significance had completely became a reality.

James Lee and Bruce Lee also shared many of the same family values. They both recognized the importance of a close family unit and openly expressed their love for their wives and children. All of their personal accomplishments aside, their families were the most important elements in their complex lives. And in this edition, we pay tribute to their greatness—both in private and in public. We have chosen to feature a few of the very personal photographs from their days together in Oakland, California—a time long past but certainly not forgotten.

. . . and that is the way history should remember James Yimm Lee and his partner Bruce Lee.

In Memoriam

James Yimm Lee

1920–1972

*"You must learn to adapt to the circumstances,
and adapt your training methods
to those circumstances."*

—James Yimm Lee
Oakland JKD Branch Sifu

In Memoriam

Bruce Lee

1940–1973

*"Using no way as way,
having no limitation as limitation."*

—Bruce Lee
Founder, jeet kune do

Beginnings

The Tiger's Humble Beginning

Before the Oakland Years...

At 8:30 in the morning on January 31, 1920, Lee Kein Heir was born at his parents' house at 927 Webster Street in Oakland, California. Although Lee Kein Heir is recorded on James' birth certificate, shortly after his birth an American name that included the original family surname was adopted. His father's real Chinese surname had been Yimm, but he had changed it to Lee for immigration purposes upon entering the United States. Lee Kein Heir would be known as James Yimm Lee, and James would always feel it was proper to include his true surname when his American name was used.

James Yimm Lee's proud parents were Lee Look On and Ching Shee Lee. James' father Lee Look On was born in San Francisco in 1880 and during his adult years established himself as a merchant by trade. For a time, Lee Look On was the proprietor of a shrimp company on Harrison Street in Oakland Chinatown. He later became a tailor and even ran a prosperous gambling house. James' mother, Ching Shee Lee, was born in China in 1880 and later immigrated to the United States and assumed the American name of Alice Lee.

The Lee family was blessed with three sons and five daughters: Jon Y. Lee, Robert Lee, James Yimm Lee, Helen (Lee) Lai, Mamie (Lee) Fong, Jennie (Lee) Lew, Mabel (Lee) Chin, and Gladys Lee, who died of polio at a young age.

James was quite close to his older brothers Jon and Robert; the oldest, Jon, was like a second father to young James and seemed to be the only one who could control him or offer him the discipline he needed when James stepped out of line or became mischievous.

All of the Lee children attended local elementary schools in Oakland and later attended the local high schools near their home. None of James' brothers or sisters showed any particular interest in athletics, being more scholastically oriented. James was the complete opposite. By the age of 10, James was beginning to excel at sports and other physical activities and had already expressed an avid interest in physical development and martial arts.

James had no intentions of going to college; he had never excelled in the scholastic academic programs offered at the grade school and high school he attended. While in his teens, he became very preoccupied with physical fitness and weightlifting and at the age of 18, while still attending Oakland Technical High School, James broke the Northern California weightlifting record in his weight class. At the time he was a member of the Oakland YMCA weightlifting team.

By the time he graduated from Oakland Technical High School in January 1939, James had won many awards for his outstanding performances in gymnastics, wrestling, and even amateur boxing. His physique had developed quite nicely and though he was only

5'6" with a very slight frame, he was highly defined. For several years after his graduation at the age of 19, James was totally engrossed with physical fitness. Many of his friends would call him nicknames such as "Shoulders" Lee, Lee the "Vee" man, or, because of his bold and confident attitude, "Tiger" Lee. By the time that James was 20, the confidence and physical abilities he had acquired through constant training prompted many of the people in Oakland Chinatown to refer to him as a real "roughneck" with a reputation for quickly defending his actions. His reputation as a rather tough kid often required him to defend himself against individuals who did not see eye-to-eye with his attitudes.

James soon realized that if he was to survive he was going to need a profession that would gain him financial independence. At the age of 20, he was accepted as an apprentice welder at the Mare Island Naval Shipyards in Vallejo, California, and began in earnest to learn a trade that would become the mainstay of his occupational career. He quickly learned the techniques of the welding trade and after working with naval ships and submarines for about one and one-half years, he began to feel the urge for travel and excitement. As the result of a request to transfer to Pearl Harbor, Hawai'i, James arrived there on December 1, 1941, just six days before the Japanese were to bomb Pearl Harbor. So it was that, at the young age of 21, James was plunged directly into the most devastating battle that ever raged in the Pacific. Before the final bombings had subsided, James, along with many other shipbuilders and welders, was immediately put to work.

For the next two and one-half years James and his co-workers worked tirelessly trying to help salvage what was left of the United States naval fleet. It was during this time that James began a serious interest in the study of martial arts. He and several of his fellow workers began to train in the arts of judo and jujitsu with the late Professor Okazaki at his martial arts gym in Honolulu. On occasions when they could not attend the classes at the school, Professor Okazaki would form special classes at the bus terminal near the workers' living quarters.

Early in June 1944, after two and one-half years of intermittent martial arts training and continual work to restore the salvaged ships, James Yimm Lee returned to Oakland to visit his family and friends. Two months later, having been involved with the war first-hand in Pearl Harbor, James was inducted into the United States Army. He and both of his brothers joined the Army to fight for their country. After a brief stint in basic training, in November 1944, James was stationed at Fort Knox, Kentucky, where he attended radio operator school. Upon completion of the necessary training, he was attached to the 716th Tank Battalion in the Philippine Islands.

During his tour of duty in the Philippines, James Yimm Lee saw plenty of action and was in combat against the Japanese at the Luzon Campaign. Although he was primarily a radio operator stationed with the tank battalion, out of necessity he also became a machine gunner. James was also engaged in the Mindanao Campaign, for which he received the Asiatic Pacific Theater Ribbon with Two Bronze Stars, the Philippine Liberation Ribbon, and the World War II Victory Medal.

James was lucky that he was never wounded in action during the fierce combative encounters, but during the latter part of the Philippine Campaign, he contracted the dreaded malaria disease. Before the close of the war, he had severe reoccurring bouts with this tropical fever, nearly dying in the intense South Pacific heat and climate. This weakened his physical condition considerably.

On January 10, 1946, he departed the Philippines for intensive medical supervision and eight days later was registered at the Letterman General Hospital in San Francisco, California. After three months of treatment and medical attention, James was released from the United States Army with an honorable discharge and 30% medical disability pay. Having seen action in the South Pacific for the duration of the war, he was awarded the rank of Private First Class and assigned to the 801st Military Police Battalion of San Francisco, California.

After returning home to Oakland, California, James resided for the next five years with his father at his home on 321 Perkins Street in Oakland. During this period, James remained a confirmed bachelor and resumed his weight training and bodybuilding to restore his health. He was determined to get in the best physical shape of his life. To sustain his livelihood he took a civilian position as an electric welder for a local firm.

During that intense five years, he and many of the close associates and friends he had before the war began to train regularly at many of the physical fitness clubs in the Oakland area. This was a very formative time in James' life.

While attending a dinner party given by one of his close friends, James Yimm Lee met a very attractive lady by the name of Katherine Margaret Chow; she would become his wife and the mother of his children.

Katherine was raised in San Jose, California, and was one of three daughters of Fannie Chow, a widow. Her sisters were Rebecca (Chow) Eastman and Esther (Chow) Louie. The Chow family had grown up on a farm in San Jose, and Katherine had attended San Jose State College for two years but had never graduated. For income, she had worked as a waitress, a Chinese cook, and a clerk-typist for the federal government and at the Naval Air Station in Alameda, California. Before meeting James, Katherine had been married twice before and had a son named Richard Jeong.

Like James, Kathy, as her close friends knew her, could speak excellent English and Cantonese dialect. They soon discovered that they had similar interests in literature, poetry, and lifestyle. After their first meeting, they began to date, soon fell in love, and were married on October 13, 1951, by the district judge of Washoe County, Nevada. James was 31 and Katherine was 28.

The following year, they were blessed with a beautiful baby girl whom they named Karena Beverly Lee. As their new home life in the Oakland area became established, it was not long before they were blessed with a second child, a son, who was born on Halloween day in 1953. They named their son Greglon Yimm Lee, forming his unusual first name by combining the names of their favorite movie stars, Gregory Peck and Marlon Brando.

Soon after Greglon's birth, the James Lee family moved to 584 Valle Vista Avenue in Oakland. During this time both James and Katherine developed new interests and hobbies; Katherine took an interest in knitting, sewing, and gardening, became involved with church activities, and even began taking professional singing lessons, eventually cutting several records. James took a fond interest in his children and spent hours at a time teaching them about the ways of nature, spending great amounts of time outdoors. In addition to bodybuilding and a renewed interest in the practice of martial arts, his first love was for his two children and his wife.

By the late 1950s, James had begun training at the Kin Mon Chinese Institute on Waverly Place in San Francisco Chinatown, under the tutelage of Professor T.Y. Wong, a noted authority in the sil lum art of Chinese gung-fu. This proved to be a very rewarding experience for James, and he spent more than three years pursuing the ancient methods of self-defense taught by Professor Wong.

By 1957, James Yimm Lee's martial arts sincerity was beginning to blossom through several outlets. He became involved in operating a weightlifting gym and began to demonstrate his physical martial arts skills in traditional techniques and martial arts weapon practice. He also began writing and publishing martial arts books and incorporated his welding skills to develop and produce unique training equipment for improving the martial arts practitioners' skills and capabilities. Although James considered many of his creative endeavors involving martial arts and physical development to be primarily a hobby, his insight and creativity were those of a true martial arts pioneer. He was never satisfied with the developments or creations that he constructed and was constantly striving to improve their performance in a way that would better suit the serious martial arts practitioner.

During this time, he authored the books titled *Fighting Arts of the Orient: Elemental Karate and Kung-Fu* and *Modern Kung-Fu Karate: Iron Poison Hand Training*. These books taught how to construct training equipment for developing and strengthening the hands and feet and demonstrated the proper training methods to prepare to break large stacks of solid bricks with one's bare hands without causing injury. A layman, with only 100 days of proper training, could perform many of the breaking techniques taught within his books.

Much of the sil lum knowledge he had learned from Professor T.Y. Wong and continued to practice was beginning to appear in print so that everyone could benefit from this knowledge.

James Lee was one of the first martial arts practitioners to give the American people an insight into the rare and ancient methods of self-defense that had previously been taught only to the Asian community.

The years spent in high school learning boxing, gymnastics, and wrestling, coupled with his experiences while learning judo and jujitsu in Hawai'i and the years training at the Kin Mon Sil Lum Gung Fu School in San Francisco Chinatown, made him a prime candidate to present this knowledge to the American people.

James Lee's creative talents extended into the mail-order book business, through which he sold many of his own publications, as well as those of other popular martial arts authors of the times. He was instrumental in supplying the guidance and advice for other aspiring martial artists who wished to publish their creative works. During these creative years, James constantly remained loyal to his family and supported them through his job as a welder but all of his additional spare time was devoted to increasing effectiveness in ways that gung-fu could be improved.

By 1958 and 1959, word had traveled far and wide that James Lee was one of the most knowledgeable martial artists in the United States, and many serious practitioners sought him out for instruction and advice. James was constantly in demand to teach his unique gung-fu skills and was often an invited guest at different functions where he was urged to perform his incredible breaking feats. These techniques were so unbelievable that most people doubted their validity until they attempted to perform the same feats. Despite his small frame, he had acquired a tremendous amount of physical power and could direct that power with a very high degree of accuracy and control. And, with his advanced knowledge of the laws of physics, he could stack a pile of solid bricks and announce which one in the stack he would break.

Word of James' martial arts abilities was so prevalent in the

Oakland area by 1959 that almost anyone who had previous experience in any style of martial arts was certain to know of James Lee in the Oakland area.

The Dragon's Rowdy Beginning

Before the Oakland Years...

On the morning of November 27, 1940, in the Chinese Year of the Dragon, Lee Jun Fan was born in San Francisco, California, under the supervision of Dr. Mary Glover. His mother, Grace Lee, had not planned on an American name for him, and his father, Lee Hoi Cheun, was performing as an entertainer in the Chinese opera that was touring the U.S. at the time, so it was Dr. Mary Glover who thought of the name Bruce. Grace Lee agreed to the name and from that time on, the child was known as Bruce Lee. Bruce was one of five children born to the Lee Hoi Cheun family. He had two brothers, Peter and Robert, and two sisters, Agnes and Phoebe.

After the completion of the Chinese opera tour, the Lee family returned to their home in Hong Kong, but not before Bruce, at the age of three months, made his first appearance as a stand-in baby in an American film titled *Golden Gate Girl*. By the time Bruce was 4, he and several of his siblings had performed as walk-on extras for a Chinese war play produced in Hong Kong. And when he was 5, at the request of the director, Bruce was offered a part in his father's latest Chinese film. From this early beginning, Bruce eventually accumulated eighteen roles in Chinese motion pictures produced in Hong Kong. This stage of his career spanned from age 5 to his mid-teens and concluded with his last child role in a film titled *The Orphan*, which was an enormous success. It was probably during these formative years that Bruce developed a liking for theatrics and acting that would follow him throughout his career.

During his childhood years, like other children of his age, Bruce developed many interests. Within the Lee family and among many of his childhood friends, he became known for the practical jokes and surprising tricks that he would play on them. When he was very small, his sister Agnes gave him the nickname "The Little Dragon"; this was a name that was to follow him into his adult years.

As time passed, much of his teenage energy began to be negatively channeled into a growing involvement with the street gangs that were becoming increasingly popular in Hong Kong at the time. He began to get in more and more street fights and it was through these combative encounters that he developed an incessant desire to win, becoming extremely furious in situations where he did fare very well.

Many of these gang-style fighting encounters occurred while he was attending La Salle College, a Catholic boys school in Hong Kong, and continued even after he had begun attending St. Francis Xavier College, a Catholic high school It was in his school years that Bruce became very "wild" and realized that out of necessity and in order to back up his verbal challenges, he should begin the study of the sophisticated self-defense system known as *wing chun*. Although Bruce had studied several other styles of self-defense (gung-fu) prior to his involvement with wing chun, he felt that this style had more to offer him for his frequent close-range encounters with Hong Kong gang members. He immediately began training under the tutelage of the wing chun master Yip Man, who at the time was the head of a style that had a lineage extending back more than 400 years. As Bruce began his training under the guidance of Yip Man, many of the fears of humiliation that had evolved from

Beginnings —

his street fighting episodes began to disappear. By the time he entered St. Francis Xavier College, he had become a proficient martial artist, as well as a rather feared bully and street fighter.

It was during these "crisis" years that Bruce expressed an avid interest in dancing and excelled in a ballroom dance style known as *cha-cha*. With his natural grace and a keen sense for picking up complicated movements and stepping patterns, he had very little difficulty in learning the dances. He spent countless hours practicing and developing the extremely complex dance routines. As a result of this positive effort, Bruce eventually became the Hong Kong Cha-Cha Champion.

During his high school years, the street fighting continued until his mother reached a point in her tolerance that she threatened to tell his father if he did not start behaving and carrying himself as he should. Because Bruce knew that his father abhorred violence of any kind and because Bruce had great respect for his father, Grace Lee figured that this method of discipline would put a halt to their child's rowdy and often-mischievous behavior. Unfortunately, this method of discipline did not work as she'd hoped and Bruce continued to engage in street fighting, even while he was playing parts in some of the Chinese motion pictures that he was appearing in at the time.

One of the brothers who was a boxing coach at St. Francis Xavier College, Brother Edward, decided that it was time to give Bruce a lesson in humility and invited him to the boxing room to put on the gloves and go a "few rounds" in a friendly match. Although Bruce had never boxed before, he held his own quite well due to his gung-fu training in wing chun. Brother Edward, undaunted, recognized Bruce's natural talent and invited Bruce to join the boxing team. He reluctantly joined but refused to train or practice in the

— **21**

conventional boxing methods. This did not seem to affect his combative skills because shortly afterward, in the school boxing tournament, Bruce defeated the boy who had been champion three years in a row. This certainly must have had an effect on Bruce Lee's later formulations that would evolve from these combative experiences.

From the time that the Hong Kong motion picture called *Orphan* was released, Bruce's popularity as an actor began to rise, and consequently, Run Run Shaw, an extremely powerful Hong Kong producer, asked him to sign an actor's contract. Bruce, having never really liked school and the rigid discipline associated with education, decided that he would quit school and accept Shaw's offer with the hopes of becoming a movie star. Although his mother was convinced that Bruce could become a star, she was fearful of what was happening to him. He was heavily involved with street fighting, movie parts, and social fraternizations, and her primary concern was to see that Bruce completed his education and received his diploma; so when he was picked up by the police for fighting, she forbade him to accept Run Run Shaw's offer. In addition, to remove him from the society that she felt was causing his downfall, Grace Lee made arrangements to send her son to the United States to finish his high school education. So it was that, in 1959, Bruce Lee boarded an American President Lines ship and set sail to America where, as his mother had hoped, he completed his high school education and then began attending the University of Washington in Seattle.

To subsidize his tuition at the university, Bruce worked as a busboy and a waiter at the popular Chinese eatery known as Ruby Chow's Restaurant. For several months he lived in the restaurant's attic in exchange for his services, but Bruce soon tired of the menial task of waiting tables. He quit the job and began teaching wing chun gung-fu, while also attending the University of Washington.

While teaching in Seattle, Bruce had the opportunity to travel to San Francisco to visit a family friend, Quan Ging Ho, an administrator of the opera. The Lee family had met him when his father was performing with the Chinese opera and he had known Bruce since his birth in San Francisco.

During his brief stay, Bruce had the opportunity to accompany Ging Ho to a house party sponsored by Brian Lum, a relative of James Yimm Lee. Bruce had just turned 20 and was well received as an old acquaintance of Quan Ging Ho. At the dinner, Bruce entertained the guests by performing gung-fu, dancing the cha-cha, and telling jokes in both Chinese and English. He was literally the life of the party and everyone was very impressed with his natural and relaxed talent and physical abilities. Word traveled throughout the Chinese communities in both Oakland and San Francisco.

Two weeks later Bruce attended a victory dance sponsored in San Francisco. The dance gave him a chance to sharpen his dancing skills while demonstrating the unique ability to perform complex dance-step arrangements that had helped him win the cha-cha championships in Hong Kong. His dancing abilities stood out among the rest of the crowd and it became apparent to many that this was the same person who had made such an impression at Brian Lum's house party a couple of weeks before.

Bob and Harriet Lee, relatives of James Yimm Lee, were in attendance at the dance, and having heard of this young Chinese dance performer, took the opportunity during an intermission to introduce themselves. So it was that, through casual conversation, the acquaintance that would become an important part of Bruce's plans for future career objectives was implemented.

Part Two

Part Two

Letters from the Past

Al Novak

"If it were not for Jim, Bruce would probably not have developed at the accelerated rate that he was moving."

I first met Jim [James Yimm Lee] at a martial arts luau where he was performing iron-hand breaking techniques. Upon our introduction, Jim asked me if I was interested in gung-fu and iron-hand training. I immediately expressed an interest in the Chinese martial arts and from then on our friendship developed. I was amazed at the brick-breaking and gung-fu skills that Jim possessed and made every effort to train as often as he would permit me at the time. I recall many times when Jim would take me to Chinatown in San Francisco, where he was training with Professor T. Y. Wong in the art of sil lum gung-fu. During these early years, Jim spent countless hundreds and hundreds of hours instructing me. It was later that I developed the skills in iron-palm training and would assist Jim in many of the breaking demonstrations that he would perform for martial arts benefits.

As our training progressed, Jim began to develop many different ways of applying the sil lum gung-fu methods with other innovative concepts that he had been formulating. Together with several other early students, we began to adapt them into our fighting styles. I suppose for that reason, many of the martial artists at that time began referring to Jim, Jack Hendricks, and myself as the "Unholy 3."

As Jim began to write books pertaining to the martial arts and iron-palm training, our friendship grew stronger and I was honored to shoot the photographs for his first martial arts books. I believe that Jimmy was really ahead of his times in many ways. Jim was responsible for writing some of the very first English versions of Chinese gung-fu martial arts books. In fact, he was probably one of the first men to demonstrate martial arts techniques on television.

It was through Jim that I had the opportunity to meet Bruce Lee. This was when Bruce first came to Oakland in 1962. As this relationship matured, Bruce, Jim, and myself would spend numerous hours at a time training and perfecting new and innovative fighting techniques. When Bruce first came to Oakland, he was really surprised that Jim was so advanced in martial arts training and I think it was through their close association that the fundamental concepts of jeet kune do were developed.

From these formulations, Jim and I began to open and operate several gung-fu schools in the Northern California area. It was in that period that the Jun Fan Gung Fu Institute was opened in Hayward, California.

Although Bruce was somewhat outspoken in his martial arts concepts, Jim was more reserved and did not talk much but when he spoke, he always had something important to say.

If it were not for Jim, Bruce would probably not have developed at the accelerated rate that he was moving. Jim was the guiding light for many of Bruce's innovative concepts, many of which the world would have never known if it was not for Jim.

In the latter part of the Oakland Years, Bruce was making contacts in Hollywood and preparing to do *The Green Hornet* while Jim was content to practice and teach martial arts in the Bay Area. Those were times when the martial arts were really getting to be quite popular. In that period of time we seemed to all be going our separate ways, but nothing can replace the knowledge that we shared in those years.

I fondly recall that when people would ask Jim what he was, Jim would boastfully reply, "I am an American." And I must add that he was a fine one at that!

George Lee

"I never will forget the teachings of Bruce and James where they were teaching me to be like bamboo and flow with the situation. Every time I see bamboo it is a reminder of those lessons."

I originally met Bruce Lee when he first came to Oakland in 1959. This was when he had first come to the United States from Hong Kong. At the time, Bruce was teaching a cha-cha class in Oakland to a group of serious dancers who met often and regularly for sessions at the dancing lodge. Bruce was teaching the classes at the time and we were quite impressed with his Chinese-style cha-cha steps and wished to learn this unique technique. Little did I realize that this brief introduction would lead to a more profound meaning and understanding of the martial arts.

When Bruce was finished with the dance instruction, after each session he would give a demonstration in wing chun gung-fu and at the same time perform some of the simplified self-defense techniques that almost anyone could learn. Since I had studied classical martial arts in China for about six years starting when I was a child of 9, and had continued to some extent during my life, I was instantly interested in what Bruce was teaching and began to inquire as to where he had learned it. I could tell that he was very proficient and had a broad background in martial arts. Not only was he good but he also carried himself in a very confident manner. We struck up a small conversation that eventually would lead to my becoming a very close friend of this young Chinese dancing champion.

For what seemed like several months, but in actuality were two or so more years, Bruce was away in Seattle, Washington, completing his education. I saw very little of him except when he would come down to visit James Lee at his home on Monticello in Oakland. Bruce would always mention that as soon as things were finished in the Seattle area he was going to move to Oakland and begin a gung-fu club and teach the serious people his style of gung-fu.

Not long after his relocation to the Oakland area did he and James open a school on Broadway in Oakland and we began to train in earnest. Looking back, I see that this was the beginning of a career for Bruce that was to be the beginning of his rise to fame

in the martial arts and motion picture industry. In those early times,
many solid friendships were forged
that would last for the better part
of over ten years.

In remembrance of those years,
there are many fond memories
and experiences that I will always
cherish. Those were times when
the martial arts were just getting

introduced into the United States and Bruce Lee and James Lee
were making history in this new era.

I am proud to have been a part of this time and felt fortunate
that I could have contributed, in a small way, toward this development.

Some of the subsequent recollections may be helpful toward
completing the picture of *Remembering the Master*, and if so, I will
have felt honored to contribute in that small way.

When Bruce and James first opened the Broadway school in
Oakland, they were highly excited about the prospect of spreading
the art of Chinese gung-fu. Although the school was relatively small,
they had very little trouble getting serious students. Bruce was very
serious as well as very professional in his approach to selecting students whom he wished to teach. He would screen each and every
student before he would accept them for enrollment. It was his
belief that if the student was serious and committed to really learning it would not be a waste of time and he further felt that no one's
time should be wasted intentionally. Bruce was very thorough in
the fact that after each student was screened for eligibility, they were
required to listen to a tape recording that he had made that

explained the purpose and reasoning behind his method of teaching. Bruce wanted every student to be educated in the principles and concepts of the yin-yang and be able to apply it to their everyday lives. I could sense that he was dead serious about his concern for the students and wanted them to possess the wisdom that is a necessary part of martial arts training.

As one of those original students, I can honestly say that I learned more in that short period than I had learned in all of my other martial arts years combined. It was only after several weeks of training at the school that I noticed that Bruce was in need of a file box to organize all of the notes and papers in the office that I decided to make one for the school. Being a machinist by trade, this was a relatively simple task. Upon its completion, I presented it to Bruce and he was genuinely impressed with the workmanship.

I suppose this marks the beginning of our close personal relationship. Both Bruce and James were pleased with the way that it was built and wanted me to build other things such as equipment and devices that would help convey the concepts of their teaching. I was delighted to build these things for the school and its members because I knew that it would help improve their skills as well as my own.

Bruce was very creative with the plans that he drew that expressed his ideas and was always coming up with new and more innovative things for me to build. Many of these pieces of equipment are still in operation in some of the schools that teach jeet kune do across the United States. When Bruce went to the Hollywood area and met new friends who were in the movies, I was delighted to build training devices for them as well.

In the early years when we were training in the Broadway school, I could see that Bruce was taking a very serious interest in bodybuilding and weight training; this was just how James had started years before. The devices that Bruce designed in that period were both simple and complicated at the same time but the challenge was always worth the satisfaction to see that certain smile on Bruce's face. Since Bruce never wanted to waste time, he had me make equipment that could keep him preoccupied with practice and exercise while he would be reading or watching television. He was always doing more than one thing at a time to get the most from an allotted amount of time. It was incredible that he could concentrate in this manner.

Since James was a welder and I a machinist, I think that we kept Bruce pretty busy coming up with new and different designs to increase his physical abilities. Both James and myself used to get a real kick out of watching Bruce come up with a new and different idea.

As the training progressed at the Oakland school, I could see that many of the techniques were evolving into a more simplified method and much of the excessive movement was eliminated. This, I would have to say, was the real beginning of the jeet kune do concepts. Many of the signs and yin-yang emblems that Bruce was designing to represent this new type of fighting concepts were reflected in the signs and models that I made for him. It was interesting to see Bruce grow and develop into a stronger and more convicted person as his concepts were becoming established.

There were times at the Oakland school that Linda Lee would come in and assist with the teaching duties. She possessed an excellent understanding of Bruce's and James' martial arts techniques and I was very impressed that she could perform and teach the way that she did. It proved to me that the new jeet kune do concepts could work just as effectively for women as they did for men. That was quite refreshing to see. Bruce was highly developed in his thoughts and methods.

The Oakland school was open about a year before it was relocated to James' home on Monticello. At that time, Bruce was beginning to make inroads and make a few connections in Hollywood so it was felt best to relocate the school back over to where James, Bruce, and Linda were living together.

During that period of time and before Bruce left for Hollywood, we were actively involved in training three times a week with a special session on Sundays. At James' home, the Sunday sessions were considered the largest of all of the classes and on many occasions, the entire garage and driveway would be crowded with people who wanted to train.

The workouts were vigorous and very serious. Bruce's sincerity was reflected in his strict discipline and he had very little patience for people who did not express complete dedication to the training. James differed considerably in this respect although he only wanted to teach the serious pupil. It was good to have diversity in training because each had a different way of presenting and teaching the many facets of jeet kune do. During the day hours while James would be at work in the welding trade, Bruce would spend the better portion of each day working out and bettering his physical ability. It did not take long before he was getting extremely muscular and taking on a well-conditioned physique. He used to show us at the beginning of each session how much he was developing and I was always flattered that he contributed his fast progress to the equipment that James and myself had made. As our friendship became stronger, there were many times when Bruce, James, and myself would frequent the restaurants in the Oakland Chinatown area.

Those were interesting times and we would spend many hours

of just chatting and telling jokes and kidding around. Bruce was a real practical joker as well as a funny comedian. Some of the jokes that they would tell made me laugh and still do so today whenever I think of them.

Even when Bruce relaxed and was kidding around he was still quite serious in his approach to martial arts. He was always writing ideas down on napkins and sometimes on tablecloths when we were dining. After the ideas had been recorded, he and James would go back to being their jovial selves.

The way that Bruce and James interacted with each other, anyone could see that they were the closest of friends and they openly spoke the way that they felt. They never held anything back from the other. Even in all of our dining experiences they were always bouncing off of one another in a way that most people could never act toward another human being. They were close, friendly, serious, jovial, joking, pulling pranks on each other, and always willing to back the other up in any type of situation.

It was always a pleasure to share in and interact with these two creative guys because they could laugh at themselves even when things did not go as they intended.

When we would leave the restaurant in Chinatown, Bruce was always testing his kicking and punching skills against any objects that were close to him. I recall that he had a favorite potted tree near one of the restaurants that he used to kick when he exited. He would kick the leaves that were head-level and cause them to fly.

He was always kicking at the parking meters along the sidewalk. Sometimes he would kick just to miss them by fractions of an inch and at other times he would make them rattle like crazy. It was a wonder that they still worked after he gave them a good kick.

There are so many times that I can recall when we shared many experiences together and it would be virtually impossible to list them all within the confines of one eulogy heading, but hopefully many of them will be listed in *Remembering the Master*. I can say, however, that James and Bruce were very close personal friends and we shared many, many moments together. They were both martial arts masters, and as Sifus they will always be my masters. They taught me much about myself and about life in general. I never will forget the teachings of Bruce and James where they were teaching me to be like bamboo and flow with the situation. Every time I see bamboo it is a reminder of those lessons. And every time I think of Bruce I think of James and every time I think of James I think of Bruce. I think they were the most compatible human beings that I have ever had the pleasure of knowing. One was a necessary component of the other and it reflected in everything that they did.

I don't think that they ever realized the effects that they were having on the world at large. Bruce would always choose his friends and I like to consider myself fortunate enough to have been one of them. I know that James was less critical of his friends but again I feel fortunate to have been one of his friends as well. Even before their untimely demise I considered James Lee as Bruce's mentor, and Bruce would have been hard pressed to tackle the movie world without the advice and guidance of James.

I still vividly recall the last time that I saw Bruce and James. It was on different occasions but each one was as if I was going to see them the next time. Bruce was celebrating his birthday in Los Angeles at his home and he was in a very happy mood. He was just getting ready to go back to Hong Kong to shoot *Game of Death*. It was shortly after that that I heard that he had died and I just could not believe it. I had thought that it was just another one of those publicity gimmicks to celebrate the beginning of the shooting of *Game of Death.* It seemed like the type of publicity that may be associated with a Bruce Lee film with a title by that name. When I realized that it was true I just went to pieces. From that time I have put martial arts out of my mind. That part of me died with Bruce.

My last conversation with James happened when he was at a service station in the Bay area. James had mentioned that he did not feel too well and he wanted to go home and relax. I knew that he was not looking too well at the time but had assumed that he was tired. He mentioned that if he just relaxed and took a bath he would probably feel fine later on. Shortly afterward, I heard that Jimmy had died and that was a total shock. It took me by surprise.

In concluding, I can say that I have lost two close and very dear friends and I will never forget the rare moments that we spent together on this earth. They were one hell of a pair of important people to me and they will never be forgotten in the body or in the spirit.

Bob Baker

"Whenever Bruce would develop new ideas, he would always confer with James before these ideas were introduced to the students of the Oakland jeet kune do school."

My first association with Bruce came while I was training with James Yimm Lee in Oakland, California. This was at the time that Bruce was still actively involved with the teaching of wing chun gung-fu.

As I began to train with James and Bruce, they were in the process of developing the concepts of jeet kune do.

Although there was twenty years' difference in age between Bruce and James, both of these men complemented each other in developing the techniques that formed the base of this fighting art. Both had perfect timing, a real understanding of the essential elements of practical fighting, in addition to the philosophical beliefs that they both shared. Bruce and James were just like the yin and yang in every respect. One counterbalanced the other's concepts in a way that the best of both sides were clearly established before a definite solution was achieved in regard to fighting techniques. Even though they complemented each other in this manner, they still shared many common interests. They both liked to create in all veins of artistic expression. They were artists, writers, fighters, philosophers, instructors, organizers, pioneers, and believers in simplicity.

They each had a mutual love and respect for the other's mental and physical abilities. This was reflected in the way that they would spend hours at a time discussing and developing new types of fighting techniques that no one had ever seen before.

I was amazed that two men could generate so much energy from one subject. On times that James, Bruce, and myself would travel together, they were always demonstrating and simplifying the foundation of jeet kune do. I recall many of the times when

Bruce would come up with new ideas, regardless of where he would be, and he would instantly get up and start practicing with me, Jim, or whomever he may be with. He would practice on planes, in the streets, restaurants, at home, movies, or wherever he would be. Bruce and James had so much energy that it was impossible for anyone to keep up with them.

In their free-time activities, I was often invited to come along, and we would spend hours at a time looking for anything that had to do with the martial arts. On occasion, we would visit bookstores, where we would search for any literary source pertaining to martial arts. Bruce collected virtually every book ever printed containing martial arts, boxing, and ancient Chinese philosophy.

Both James and Bruce were exceptionally fond of Chinese philosophy and they were well versed in the teachings of Lao Tzu and the I'Ching as well as other great philosophers. In fact, it was not uncommon for them to quote these early teachers when they were formulating many of the concepts of jeet kune do.

Bruce and James were very particular about their beliefs about life in general and it showed when they were expressing their ideas on the subject.

I feel honored to have contributed to the martial arts library that Bruce began and it was probably because of his broad background in martial arts literary study that put him ahead of his times.

Whenever Bruce would develop new ideas, he would always confer with James before these ideas were introduced to the students of the Oakland jeet kune do school.

For the three years that Bruce spent in the Oakland area, while living at James' house, I had the opportunity to be with Bruce and on many occasions, I would spend ten to fourteen hours a day practicing at the school or at James' house. These were times where

Bruce was changing from day to day and it was incredible that one man could grow so much in a short span of only three years. In those training sessions where I worked out with Bruce I never had to worry about being careful; we could both take a punch or give a punch or kick and in many instances I went down. We never worried about serious injury and that is probably the reason that progress was made at such a great pace. James used to get a big kick out of watching me practice with Bruce and although I was not always the best competition for Bruce, he felt that I could handle myself against most martial artists of the times.

I began to realize that all the training sessions that we were involved in were actually the beginning of the jeet kune do concepts. From this point of view, I really learned a lot about the fighting arts and myself.

I suppose it was from these intense classes that Bruce realized that I had more potential than I thought that I had, and both Bruce and James encouraged me to reach deeper into myself than I had ever gone before. As the Oakland jeet kune do school opened, I think that only a few of the serious students really realized what they had in having Bruce and James as instructors. As with everything, many do not realize what they have until it is gone. I am sure now that most of those early students realize what a privilege it was to have had these great men as instructors.

From those early beginnings, I came to appreciate the concepts of simplicity conveyed through Bruce's and James' teachings. At the Oakland school, the concepts were expressed in terms of simplified motion, and I am sure that many of the earlier students were probably looking for more than what was taught.

Bruce and James used to teach that highly complicated problems could be solved with simple solutions. This is in essence the concept taught through jeet kune do. Become evasive without blocking; emphasize offensive tactics, and use blocking as offensive maneuvers. This concept can be applied to virtually every facet of one's daily life.

"Always be willing to adapt to the times" is what Bruce used to say and I still practice that in my daily life.

James became like a father and Bruce became like a brother. I consider myself very fortunate to have had them as very good friends and close personal acquaintances. They touched my life very deeply and hardly a day passes that I do not think about them and the many experiences that we shared.

Bruce was responsible for getting me into several of the films that were being produced in Hong Kong and I really appreciated the role that I played with him in one of the earlier films. I dedicated my last film entitled *Valley of the Double Dragon* to him.

I will never forget all of the demonstrations and training sessions that we performed together.

In concluding, I honestly believe that Bruce needed the Oakland Years. Without Oakland, its students, and friends, I do not think that jeet kune do would have come about. The Oakland class was very important to him.

Allen Joe

"Bruce and James were so interested in so many of the same things you would think that they were struck from the same mold."

I first met James in about 1935 when we were students together at Lincoln Grade School in Oakland, California. It was not until 1962 that I had the opportunity to meet Bruce.

In the earlier years, James and I became really good friends and participated in many sporting activities together. In our teenage years we got involved with bodybuilding and several styles of classical gung-fu.

Even in those days, James was constantly trying to improve bodybuilding methods and certain styles of fighting arts. As partners, we trained regularly and it was with James' help and constant drive that I won Mr. Northern California in 1946. I honestly believe that James was one of the very first bodybuilders to implement program training for weightlifting. James was a real pioneer in that area. In fact, James was the person responsible for introducing Bruce Lee to bodybuilding. Even before James got into bodybuilding, he was a tremendous street fighter. He was like a bull! Looking back, I see the same similarities in Bruce: both were street fighters, both were martial artists, and both were interested in weight training. It is uncanny that the similarities are that close.

It was at the request of James, when I went to the Seattle World's Fair in Washington, that I met Bruce for the first time. At that time Bruce was teaching wing chun gung-fu and had a very avid interest in martial arts of all kinds. As an intermediary, I believe it was through this meeting that James and Bruce became good friends and workout partners.

When Bruce moved to Oakland, he lived with James for several years and during that time many of the concepts of jeet kune do were formulated. Bruce and James were so interested in so many of the same things you would think that they were struck from the same mold. I was even more surprised when James began writing martial arts books. Even in that respect both James and Bruce were so much alike. Those men were true pioneers in martial arts development.

Bruce, James, and myself used to spend hours and hours just talking about the philosophies of the martial arts and how they applied to everyday life in general. I think that many of Bruce's concepts derived from those lengthy sessions.

The experiences that we shared together will never be forgotten and I wish they were still here. Just to reminisce of those Oakland Years brings back many memories of the things that Bruce, James, and myself used to do together.

Seemingly simple things—like working out together, dining out at the different restaurants, picking up Bruce at the Oakland airport when he came up from Hollywood, telling jokes, teaching students at the school, or just being together for the sake of friendship—mean so much when you miss these great guys.

It is hard to put into words all of the experiences that we had the chance to share because there were so many and so little time.

Felix Macias, Sr.

"Bruce was a very gifted and talented individual who dedicated his life to hard work, while James was oftentimes the guiding light for many of Bruce's original ideas and jeet kune do concepts."

It was several years prior to 1964 that my interest in the martial arts began to develop. I had visited several schools but was not overly impressed with the way in which self-defense was being taught. Many of the existing schools at the time were teaching in a very formal and regimented fashion with most of the emphasis placed on the rigid traditional standards.

Then in 1964, a friend mentioned that there was a Chinese gentleman by the name of James Yimm Lee who was teaching the art of Chinese gung-fu at the Haymont Shopping Center in Hayward, California. The school was named the "Chinese Gung Fu Center." He demonstrated several extremely quick hand combinations and I was tremendously impressed with his knowledge of the fighting arts. James Yimm Lee agreed to accept me as a student and I immediately began training with him.

As I became more acquainted with James, I began to travel to his home on Monticello Avenue in Oakland for additional training. It was in that same year that I was introduced to Bruce Lee, who was training with James in the garage of the Monticello home.

At the time, little did I know that this meeting would change my life and outlook toward the martial arts. These two men could perform *chi sao* (sticking hands) wing chun drills like nobody I have seen since.

Both James and Bruce were the perfect complement for each other's martial art skills. It was during the years that I trained with James and Bruce that the jeet kune do principles and concepts were developing out of the "simplification" and combining of these two great men's fighting skills. As a regular student, I had the opportunity to learn many of these new evolving principles firsthand. These two men were like scientists experimenting with all types of "realistic" self-defense and fighting techniques and I was fortunate enough to be on the ground floor of all of these new and innovative concepts.

Throughout the time I was training with James and Bruce, my ideas on life and simple practicality began to change and I began to look at James as a father figure and Bruce as a brother. Bruce was a very gifted and talented individual who dedicated his life to hard work, while James was oftentimes the guiding light for many of Bruce's original ideas and jeet kune do concepts.

As these new concepts began to emerge and a fuller picture of the concepts was taking shape, Bruce's personality became more dynamic and his ability to express himself became more direct. This was also reflected in his martial arts techniques, which were becoming more streamlined, and it seems that he was getting quicker with the passing of each and every day.

Bruce and James were an inseparable team while they were together in the Oakland Years. They shared a zest for life and a commitment for perfection in their martial arts endeavors.

Looking back at those formative years, I still see developments that they contributed to the world as unsurpassed even by today's standards.

I also remember the Oakland Years as being very important in creating many of the unique pieces of training equipment that Bruce would design and James would construct.

I always knew that Bruce was going to be the biggest martial arts box office attraction the world has ever known when he began the role of "Kato" in *The Green Hornet* television series. There was no stopping this man. I remember Bruce always calling James to ask advice on business matters that were happening in Hollywood. This really reaffirmed my belief that these two men were very close and more than just friends.

Bruce and James were creative and original in virtually every aspect of the martial arts—their techniques, concepts, philosophical beliefs, their training equipment, and training methods. I feel really fortunate that I have shared the times together with them, and I'm trying to carry on their teachings of jeet kune do in the way that both James and Bruce would have liked.

For those of us who had the good fortune to really know Bruce and James, and have had our lives partially shaped by them, their passing is saddening beyond words. It has brought out my awareness more than anything that I can think of in regard to martial arts. I will always cherish the times and memories that occurred in the Oakland Years. The original books that were written by Bruce and James and given to me are and will always be cherished mementos of those great years.

Jasper Cummings

"It looked like Bruce was a sponge absorbing all kinds of things where James was a truck driving straight through!"

I first met James Lee in Oakland at the 10th Street and Franklin Avenue Weightlifting Gym. This was in the earlier part of the 1960s. It was just through coincidence that we struck up a conversation while in a weightlifting session. Essentially our meeting stemmed from a conversation when I inquired as to what James did in the line of sports, because he was extremely built for a man of his size. James conveyed that he was very interested in weightlifting and practiced the Chinese art of gung-fu. As our first conversation ensued about our mutual interest—his in gung-fu and mine in judo—it became obvious that we had a similar interest in these fields. I expressed to James that I had an interest in learning to use the yawara stick since I was actively involved in law enforcement. I was further surprised that James could use the yawara stick, and I immediately began training at his home on Monticello Avenue in Oakland, California.

During the period of about one year, I trained with James continuously three times per week and was constantly amazed with the broad assortment of martial arts knowledge that this man possessed. I was introduced to Sil Lum forms, fighting techniques, iron-palm training, and many forms of punching methods. It was incredible that a man of this size possessed the power and speed. James Lee could perform breaking feats that I have never seen another human being perform.

I could see that James was a determined individual with a strong desire to apply power lifting and other forms of weight training into his martial arts methods. I believe that he was the first man who studied martial arts that utilized this concept. James left a very strong impression with me for some of the feats that he could perform by combining these principles. I remember seeing him take a 100-pound dumbbell and bring it to his shoulders and push it over his head eight or nine times without exerting much effort at all.

He could strike a heavy bag filled with lead shot and just make that bag quiver and shake. He hit with so much power and focus that it sounded like bones crushing. With his hands and arms, it was as though his bones and flesh were one.

James always expressed to me that nothing was impossible if one set their mind to accomplish it. He went so far beyond what I had seen other people do with the martial arts that it was utterly incredible. He pushed himself like no other human being that I had seen. I think that he accomplished this by utilizing techniques that evolved from a very tight control of the anger that must be felt to reach such peaks.

The times that we spent in the garage at James' home were some of the most profitable times that I have ever experienced in understanding the mental and physical relationships of a person's being. James was a true martial artist and a very dangerous man if he wanted to be. I would rather attempt to kick a rattlesnake than try to attack him.

I was really glad that he was a friend of mine. James was a very likeable and softhearted person even though he never showed that side too often. He appeared to me like a person who had a temper that was right on the edge. From this quality, he could will his body to do anything that he wanted it to do. There was absolutely nothing that this man couldn't do with martial arts skills.

The first time that I met Bruce Lee, he appeared very cocky and self-assured. I felt that Bruce was a strongly determined individual who learned much from James Lee. James was older and more experienced than Bruce, and I think it was for this reason that Bruce appreciated James' skills and martial art abilities. James was very impressive even to Bruce. I can't help thinking that anyone who met and practiced with James would be impressed by his skills. It was during this time that I saw Bruce change many of his techniques and move more in the direction of James. It's easy to see why Bruce would want to do this to increase his overall fighting skill. Bruce really respected James in many ways.

They were at opposite ends of the spectrum in many physical characteristics. Bruce had a floating quality with lots of grace to his movements whereas James was solid as iron. It looked like Bruce was a sponge absorbing all kinds of things where James was a truck driving straight through!

In my year of training with James, he taught me much about myself. I do not think James wanted to instill within me a large body of knowledge but to instill the individual ability to accomplish through the mind, will, and focus of energies. He gave me the ability to realize that nothing was impossible and went beyond what other people try to teach with martial arts practice.

The last time that I had the opportunity to see James was about three months before his book release. That was at the time that Al Novak and myself were taking pictures for James' book. James was a very impressive individual.

Ed Kim Yee

"During the training sessions with Sifu Jimmy, while I was making strong attacks, he would be unbuttoning my shirt with one hand while defending with only one hand. He was very impressive."

My Sifu, James Yimm Lee, was one of the greatest men I have ever met. He was soft-spoken, gentle, and extremely proficient in the art of Chinese gung-fu. In recalling the Oakland Years, I could see why no one would ever want to mess with Sifu James. He was a very powerful man who had mastered the art of self-defense.

I was introduced to James in the early 1960s through a mutual friend by the name of George Rodriguez. We met at James' home on Monticello in Oakland and soon after I began to train in the art of wing chun gung-fu. Sifu Jimmy began me on a specialized training program that included, for the most part, private lessons. These sessions usually lasted about twenty minutes in duration but they were extremely helpful because they were intense and directed toward individual progression. His teachings were centered on simplicity and the conservation of energy. James used to always stress the importance of simplicity and incorporated that knowledge into the "basic four corner" defense that he taught. He also taught me the "one-arm defense" that worked very well for me. I learned the principles of the "three S's" that Jimmy deemed important to the study of martial arts. Essentially, the three S's were different sizes, different shapes, and different strengths. These principles were taught in such a manner that I could apply my self-defense skills to a variety of situations without modifying my style.

One of the greatest experiences I had with Sifu was in a lesson in close-range fighting techniques. When he taught me the one-arm defense/offense fighting, he would insist that I attack him in any way that I would like without pulling the punches or kicks. I could not touch him. During those training sessions, while I was making strong attacks, he would be unbuttoning my shirt with one hand while defending with only one hand. He was very impressive.

As our training progressed, he presented me with many ideas on specialized training equipment that I constructed from his plans. This equipment really helped my gung-fu training.

In the last days of Sifu's life, he presented me with some advanced training apparatus that he used in training.

Sifu James was a great gung-fu man.

George Tom

"With the martial arts movie image that Bruce had acquired through hard work and determination, very few people are really aware that James Lee had a lot to do with Bruce's success."

I was originally introduced to James Lee while attending junior high school with his son Greglon Lee. I had heard mention that

Mr. Lee taught the Chinese art of gung-fu in his home and soon after I began to visit Greglon at his home, where I would casually observe his father teaching students in the garage area. At first, I was not as fascinated with the martial arts as I was with the unique training devices that James had constructed for the purpose of developing the students' combative skills. These apparatus were totally unique in construction and design and one could see that much thought and planning had gone into their construction.

It was in about 1970 that myself and a small group of close friends began to take a more serious interest in the Chinese art of gung-fu and started to train on a regular basis. At this time, James Lee was teaching jeet kune do and the training was very direct. The linear punching and low-level kicking techniques could be directed to the training devices, and a very realistic feel could be developed for making contact with a firm object. James Lee was always stressing the importance of physical conditioning and bodybuilding to increase our abilities.

Although the memory of these past times seems to be a bit fragmented in context, there are some specific remembrances that come to mind in regards to this gentleman.

As an instructor, James Lee was very direct and took the martial arts training very seriously. He had no time for someone who was indecisive toward committing themselves to serious study.

I vividly recall him saying, "Either you come to class or you don't come to class . . . either you do or you don't." He didn't waste time in letting someone know how he felt about training. As blunt as it may have seemed to someone, he was very direct in his approach to teaching and he wanted everyone who trained to learn from his experiences.

On one occasion I remember Bruce dropping by the Monticello

home and he stood quietly at the top of the stairs leading into the garage and casually observed a class in session. James Lee stopped the class and introduced the well-developed gentleman as Bruce Lee and everybody in the class got to meet him for the first time. After class, Bruce used what we had been learning and we mentioned that we had been working with kicking techniques. Suddenly, Bruce asked if we could do the side-kick, as he

commenced to execute a quick and sharply directed side-kick straight up and to the side of his body. This he performed without even leaning over to readjust his balance. He was incredibly quick and his movements were clean and precisely focused.

Later, Bruce said that he wished all of his students had the desire and sincerity that we had, when he was living in Oakland.

One of the most important aspects of training that I learned from James Lee, as well as indirectly by Bruce Lee, was the philosophy by which they taught. This philosophy can be applied to everyday life and used to enhance one's understanding of themselves. One should be able to change and flex with each different situation confronted in life. No matter what you learn in the beginning and what you learn in the end, you must be able to change and adapt to meet each obstacle. There may be times when you have to be innovative and go for it on your own. One should always be fluid and not rigid.

James Lee and Bruce Lee seemed to represent this philosophy very well.

With the martial arts movie image that Bruce had acquired through hard work and determination, very few people are really aware that James Lee had a lot to do with Bruce's success. They could not be separated.

In eulogy, James Lee was unique in many ways but perhaps the thing that stands out most importantly to me was the fact that he was very open-minded and willing to share his knowledge. He was one who would share with all races and not just with the Chinese, as was traditional for centuries past. He was very liberal in his actions and deeds.

I see Bruce Lee as a symbol representing the acceptance of a culture that was kept secretive for so many centuries. Bruce Lee was responsible for opening up the martial arts to the world.

Leo Fong

"I realize that James and Bruce were great teachers. They did not insist we punch and kick just like them. They gave us the concept, and we were to develop our own identity."

I first met James Yimm Lee in 1960 at the Kin Mon Chinese Gung Fu Club, on Waverly Place in San Francisco Chinatown. I had just

begun my training in gung-fu
at that time, and was slumming
one Saturday evening around
the different gung-fu clubs in
Chinatown to get firsthand
knowledge of the different styles
and methods. When I walked
into the Kin Mon Club, there
were only three people training.
My attention fell on a lonely figure in a far corner of the club.
He was executing movements
with the intensity of a boxer
who is determined to win a
championship.

After he had finished his series of gung-fu movements, he pro-
ceeded to the opposite corner of the room, picked up a couple of
dumbbells, and repeated the previous movements he had done
without weights. I was impressed by his total commitment to the
training session. I waited until he was through to talk to him. I
was impressed by his dedication to the art, but more impressed
by his knowledge of the martial arts. From that day on, I made
every effort to visit with James. The highlight of my association
with James came in the mid-'60s when he invited me to meet a
young and cocky gung-fu practitioner by the name of Bruce Lee.
After my meeting, I became an official student of both James and
Bruce. By then, James' concept of the fighting arts had moved from
classical to nontraditional because of his interest in the practical
aspect of fighting. Bruce introduced James to wing chun, a more
practical approach to combat. One of the things that impressed

me about James was the ease in which he made the transition. From that day forward, he was totally committed to practical application and Bruce Lee's philosophy of spontaneous expression.

Bruce felt that pre-arranged patterns such as those in *kata* and other traditional systems were stifling to one's aliveness. Effective fighting is the ability to express one's techniques like a sound and an echo. James Lee was able to pick this up and communicate it to his students. I am fortunate to have been the beneficiary of his newfound knowledge, even though it was only for a couple of years. Now as I look back, I realize that James and Bruce were great teachers. They did not insist we punch and kick just like them. They gave us the concept, and we were to develop our own identity. What came out was ours, and each technique expressed had our own individual trademark, rather than just a clone of the instructors. This was what made James an outstanding teacher and martial artist. Khalil Gibran summarized it for us when he said: "If he [teacher] is indeed wise he does not bid you enter the house of his wisdom, but rather leads you to the threshold of your own mind. For the vision of one man lends not its wings to another man. ..." James Lee was the profile of a dedicated martial artist. His every waking moment was devoted to making martial arts an effective vehicle for self-improvement.

Any development in my own personal life must be credited to James and Bruce Lee for giving me the seed and the concept. This philosophy has helped me to be self-reliant and innovative in other areas of life. I can think of nothing more stifling than waiting for the instructor to give you his vision and his knowledge. The key to growth is taking responsibility for your own development, and to nurture that which is within. The teacher can only point the way, but it is the student who takes the responsibility to enter. I credit James Lee for *pointing the way.* The experience I gained from him was invaluable in my development also as a martial artist. The tribute to James through this book is long overdue. He was truly a dedicated martial artist.

Gary Cagaanan

"There is no question that Jimmy played a most significant role in Bruce's development as a martial artist!"

When I first learned that a book was being written about Jimmy Lee and his relationship with Bruce Lee, I felt a great sense of satisfaction in that Jimmy was to finally attain his rightful plaudits as a true pioneer in jeet kune do.

Jimmy was never the type of individual to yearn for the limelight. Even during Bruce's heyday, Jimmy more or less chose to sit back and take pride in Bruce's success, a success that he, in many ways, contributed to.

Years ago, my personal interest in the martial arts was spawned when I first saw Bruce in the role of "Kato" in *The Green Hornet* television series. Soon thereafter, I saw an ad in a magazine advertising Bruce Lee's book titled *Chinese Gung-Fu: The Philosophical Art of Self-Defense.* Without hesitation, I sent my money and received a copy. It was crudely written but contained the information that I was seeking. Even today, this book is very rare and is considered a collector's item by now.

On the back cover, a simple note was written that stated that if I was interested in lessons, to call the number. I called the number numerous times but never got an answer. Discouraged, I quit calling. Little did I know, at the time, that the number was Jimmy Lee's home telephone number.

Soon thereafter, I began my training in traditional gung-fu. Although I was what you could call a loyalist to the style that I was studying then, I was nevertheless intrigued by what I had been reading in martial arts publications about Bruce's nontraditional ideas. Bruce's theories and concepts, radically different from what I had been taught previously, stirred my thoughts. Objectively and realistically, Bruce's concepts and thoughts made sense to me.

During those early years, Bruce was adamant about never going commercial, i.e. opening a chain of martial art schools, which no doubt would have been very successful since he was riding the crest of success both as a martial artist and as an actor. I thought about how unfortunate it was that his teachings would be just about impossible to experience or learn firsthand because of that.

Then one day, as if designed by fate, I encountered an individual named Howard Williams, who really started me down the path to changing my perspectives on the martial arts.

I was sitting in a science class, drawing a picture of the yin-yang symbol on a piece of scratch paper, not paying any attention to the lecture, when the drawing caught Howard's eye. Naturally, a discussion about the martial arts ensued. Howard's dialogue seemed strangely parallel to that of which I'd read in the past writings about jeet kune do. When Howard finally revealed that he was a student of Jimmy Lee, I couldn't believe my ears.

Howard agreed to introduce me to Jimmy. But first I was eager to qualify his knowledge and/or ability in jeet kune do. Howard

always verbalized simplicity and directness in technique, combining the essences of speed and power.

Once he demonstrated, I was an instant convert. Simple, direct, fast, and powerful. I had seen many fine martial artists up to that point, but what Howard showed me sort of blew me away. It can easily be argued that Howard was one of the best to ever come out of the Oakland branch.

My first meeting with Jimmy was at his home. Though not large in size, he was powerfully built. What really impressed me, however, was his ability to interpret or explain Bruce's philosophy to me in a convincing fashion. Jimmy not only explained things well but he actually showed me as well.

For example, when demonstrating JKD, Jimmy would say, "Throw a punch," or "Throw a kick." When I did so, he easily defended against it and adapted to it. It was so natural, so fluid. He never said to throw a specific punch or kick, such as a jab, a hook, or sidekick. He was able to adapt to any strike or combination with natural ease. That is the beauty of jeet kune do.

There was no fancy storefront to signal the whereabouts of the Oakland JKD branch. Only a fortunate few knew of its location and even fewer were fortunate enough to be able to train there. Aside from the ingenious training equipment developed by Jimmy, there was nothing fancy about the Oakland school. The workouts held in the garage of Jimmy's home were, aside from a traditional show of respect for the instructor, nontraditional and informal.

Punching and kicking—with an emphasis on speed, power, footwork, rhythm, reflexes, fluidity, and economy of movement—took the place of the traditional emphasis placed on stances, forms, and pre-arranged sparring sessions. As Bruce always said, "You can't learn to swim on dry land."

Training under Jimmy was almost like being trained under the watchful eye of a seasoned fight manager. Jimmy had all of the guile and cunning of a veteran trainer and he had the keen ability to spot flaws or weaknesses in a student's execution.

Through Jimmy, I had come full circle as a martial artist. I learned that there was no such thing as an ultimate martial art. I learned that more often than not, a martial art is only as good as the person practicing it, and that one's personal development as a martial artist supersedes the study of any particular style or method.

Through Jimmy, I learned that physical combat is as precarious as any physical sport or activity. For example, it is often said that football is a "game of inches." Unarmed combat is very much the same way. The difference between victory and defeat could easily be a lucky punch or kick, the ability to absorb a blow (or land one), and on and on.

What Bruce and Jimmy emphasized was realism. The realities of combat, the honing of one's tools, and conditioning. Their goal? To strip a student down to the bare essentials needed to defend oneself effectively, to open a student's mind to anything that is useful, and to do away with what is not.

In Jimmy Lee, Bruce could not have asked for a finer disciple. There is no question that Jimmy played a most significant role in Bruce's development as a martial artist.

The ingenious training devices that Jimmy developed for Bruce certainly proved beneficial, especially in light of the fact that they held up under the brutal punishment that Bruce was capable of dealing out in a training session. Training partners would not have been able to withstand such punishment. Jimmy flatly stated that "Bruce could kill a man with one punch or kick." As a witness to the man's incredible speed and power, I certainly had no reason to doubt him.

Perhaps what Bruce valued the most about Jimmy was the friendship they shared. Jimmy served as an effective, articulate, and influential spokesman and representative of JKD. The friendship that they shared, however, extended beyond the boundaries of instructor and student, or between two martial artists. It was apparent when I saw them together. It was family!

A brief discussion with Bruce that I remembered further gave credence to it all. I remembered that I was very hesitant to tell Bruce that I was boxing in college while also training in JKD. I feared that he would be disappointed or angry that I would consider practicing another form of combat while learning JKD. Instead, his reaction was the total opposite. He actually said, "Good for you, Gary!" and he even encouraged me to keep it up. Bruce always liked boxing, I suppose, because it was "real."

Bruce and Jimmy always discouraged us from limiting our scope or perspective. They always taught us to be open, yet skeptical, and to be ourselves when "expressing" ourselves in combat. In JKD, everything is everything!

With the likes of Jimmy Lee's son, Greg, and partner, Felix Macias, JKD is alive and well once again in Oakland, and it is hoped that the tradition set forth by the old Oakland JKD branch will continue as always.

Finally, I would like to dedicate my contribution to this book to my former training mates, namely, Curtis Yee, Edward Yee, Professor Stan Piasik, Howard Williams, Richard Carney, my current Escrima instructor, Santiago (Sonny) Unpad, and the many others I had the pleasure of training with who are far too numerous to mention.

Jim Wong

"James used to say, 'The atom bomb is useless without a delivery system.... So you have to learn timing and movement to get in to the opponent.... That's your delivery system!'"

I began gung-fu training with James Yimm Lee in 1968 and continued until about 1970. At the time, I was attending Laney Junior College in Oakland, but later when I transferred to San Francisco State College it became very difficult to continue my training.

A mutual friend first introduced me to James by the name of Gilbert Yuen, who was a student at the time. Gilbert used to demonstrate some incredible hand techniques that were quick and very direct. These were techniques that I could see would be very effective in self-defense situations.

I suppose the influence that Bruce Lee had on me while demonstrating gung-fu on *The Green Hornet* television series prompted my interest to begin training. When I found out that James and Bruce were training partners, I wanted to get involved and learn this art. When I was introduced to James Lee at his home in Oakland, I was only going to learn for several months, but the classes were so direct and the knowledge was so abundant that my time of training extended almost two and one-half years. I really got caught up in it!

Since there were only ten to twelve students in a class, there was a lot of personalized attention and this impressed me very much.

Most of the martial arts schools at the time were teaching in a strict and regimented manner with very little in the way of realistic training methods, but James Lee used every type of training device imaginable to create a very realistic environment for developing our fighting techniques.

I had never seen so many types of training apparatus and punching devices in operation. You could make full contact and feel the results from the equipment. The low-level kicks and direct punching made a lot of sense to me and I really liked the realistic contact.

I was really impressed with Bruce Lee when we first met but my first observation was that he was a bit "cocky," but he was good and could back up what he said. He was a very agile person and could kick high and fast even though he did not teach those techniques in class. He used to say, "It's good to be able to have that control over the body because it makes the practical techniques easier to do." He was highly defined from the physical conditioning, and the muscles in his stomach and arms were extremely developed. He used to say, "The muscles of the stomach area should always be in condition in the event that the opponent gets in a lucky punch." He was always prepared for all types of eventualities.

I remember Bruce demonstrating his incredible kicking speed. He would tell me to extend a hand outward away from the body and he would attempt to kick it before I could move it. He would kick it so fast that I never saw his foot move from the floor. He was very quick and had outstanding reflexes to know what an opponent may be thinking or when he would move.

Bruce would say, "The secret to jeet kune do is timing and reflexes and to use them to the best advantage to suit each particular situation." He could sure practice what he preached.

Both James and Bruce placed a great deal of importance on timing and reflexes. The timing required to get in to an opponent and get out before the opponent knows what has happened is crucial to every fighting situation regardless of what one knows. The equipment really helped toward gaining a real understanding of real balance when contact is made with an opponent. James would say, "You cannot expect to hit air and have a good understanding of balance. You have to hit something to know the difference between realistic balance and false balance."

They taught the realistic approaches to practical self-defense. I recall Bruce and James' approach to fighting against opponents who used knives or guns. They would teach that the best defense was to get out of the way. This was a lot different than what most schools were teaching at the time. Most of the schools were teaching intricate techniques to disarm the opponent. Bruce and James did not believe in this approach at all.

When James would teach the importance of timing and getting in and getting out, especially when one was skilled at punching and understanding how to use timing, he would say, "The atom bomb is useless without a delivery system.... So you have to learn timing and movement to get in to your opponent.... That's your delivery system!"

Although I have never had to use my self-defense skills in an actual confrontation, the lessons learned from Bruce and James in their teachings have always been applied to other areas of my daily life. The method of learning that they taught works so well in every facet of daily life.

Even the processes of realistic evaluations help one to gain a clear understanding of the processes that should be used to learn any subject regardless of the contents.

As a eulogy, I thought both Bruce Lee and James Yimm Lee were very peaceful people who had a high amount of respect for the other. People were always trying to get them to prove themselves. James had a solid respect for Bruce, and Bruce had a solid respect for James. They were willing to share their knowledge with any-one who was interested and would listen to them.

I think that Bruce and James were true believers in the real gung-fu philosophy and that is what they were teaching.... It was their religion and they wanted to make people aware of it by spreading the word.

Robert Garcia, Jr.

"James used to teach me by saying, "Make your hands as strong as your feet and make your feet as fast as your hands, then make it all one form of motion.""

I first met James Yimm Lee in 1970 when I became interested in learning the martial arts. I had heard through a friend that James was very good and decided to visit his home on Monticello Avenue in Oakland in hopes of joining his class. Upon meeting him, I said that I was interested in learning martial arts. I was dismayed when he replied that he didn't teach karate and suggested that I find another place that taught. He also mentioned that he taught "a form of scientific street fighting" and that I would not be interested in this form of self-defense. In essence, I recall that he actually tried to discourage me from beginning his style of Chinese gung-fu. After I said that a mutual friend recommended me, he accepted me as a student and I immediately began training in wing chun gung-fu, which gradually led to my development in jeet kune do.

In the next two years, I trained regularly and had the opportunity to learn many of the concepts that were still being developed pertaining to jeet kune do.

I recollect that James was a very religious man even though he did not have a steady religion. This was reflected in the way that he treated people and was always obliging their needs. We would take long walks and discuss many philosophical topics related to life in general and how they applied to the study of martial arts.

He gave me much insight as to the way that personal observations fitted into the art of jeet kune do.

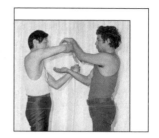

He used to quote many of the sayings from Shakespeare and compare them to contemporary life. One of his favorite quotes came from *Macbeth*, Act 5, Scene 5. To him, this really made sense of what life was all about.

Last year, James mentioned to me on several occasions that his time on earth was getting short and he felt that he could sense the end.

It was during some of the last training sessions that he began to really stress achieving the maximum proficiency from the efforts that I exerted. One of the things pertaining to jeet kune do that I vividly recall was when he said, "Make your hands as strong as your feet and make your feet as fast as your hands, then make it all one form of motion."

In those fleeting moments that we spent together, James taught me more than martial arts and for that I will always be indebted.

Ernest Benevidez

"I was not overly impressed with Bruce Lee until he went into action and began demonstrating his fantastic martial arts skills."

The first time that I ever spoke with James Yimm Lee was over the telephone. At that time, I had trained in the art of kenpo for a period of about one year and was seeking knowledge that went beyond the formal training that I was receiving at the time.

I had heard of James through several acquaintances, but they had mentioned that this Chinese gung-fu teacher would not accept non-Asian students and I decided to call to confirm this fact. Upon talking to James Yimm Lee, he could not believe that rumors of this nature were being passed around the martial arts community, and he invited me to come over to his home in Oakland if I was truly interested in training in Chinese gung-fu.

At my very first meeting with James, I was quite impressed with his knowledge of the combative arts. Not only was he skilled in several styles, but also was rather progressive in concepts of applying boxing and street fighting that he taught to his students. I immediately began training with James and Al Novak, who was also teaching at James' house. I could not help noticing that James was one of the most progressive Asian human beings that I had ever met.

It was a short time after I began training that I met Bruce Lee at James' house. This was at a workout session.

I was not overly impressed with Bruce Lee until he went into action and began demonstrating his fantastic martial arts skills. Both he and James could execute "lightning fast" techniques that were not pre-arranged and perform techniques or countermaneuvers without thinking or pre-planning their movements.

During the early parts of my training, I was taught the necessary elements of the sil lum style and then introduced to the forms of wing chun. Within the first year I had begun to realize that James and Bruce were methodically cutting away at the superficial movements and getting to the pure, "raw" essence of fighting. As this transformation was taking place, the small group of serious students including myself was developing at a greater rate of speed than ever before.

I recall very vividly how Bruce and James conducted some of the most rugged training that I had ever experienced and I understood why many of the not-so-serious students dropped out after only a very short period of time. James used to say, "If a student does not have a warrior soul, he should not be studying martial arts in the first place." These early lessons have helped me in everything that I have ever experienced since that time.

At both the Broadway school and at the garage at James' home, Bruce and James were always creating new and innovative concepts in ways to make fighting more effective. All the time, this new knowledge was passed on to the students.

The more the art of jeet kune do evolved, the more that Bruce and James would speak of the outdated classical styles of martial arts. Bruce became quite fond of saying, "Give me a street fighter that knows how to box and with our jeet kune do, I'll teach him to waste a black belt in six months."

Although Bruce and James were totally committed to the martial arts, they were both very compassionate men. And in time, through my training and friendship, I came to respect James in the same manner as a father and looked upon Bruce as a very close personal friend. I would have done anything for those men in a moment. In recalling some of the earlier days, Bruce wore glasses when he would practice, and I asked him how he could see if someone got in close and knocked the glasses off.

Bruce realized this as a disadvantage and soon after, I made him several sets of contact lenses that he began to wear when he trained. It was later that I made him twelve sets of different ones to be used for some of his movie projects. When Bruce became popular as a movie star, I made him a set of green contact lenses that he could wear to disguise his appearance. When he changed his hairstyle and wore the green ones, it was impossible to pick him out in a crowd. When they were in the process of working on *The Silent Flute*, I made him a set of white opaque lenses that would give him the appearance that he was completely blind. This was supposed to be for his role in the movie.

In recalling many of the earlier experiences, the more I see that James and Bruce were like two trains intersecting at the same time. They were so far ahead of their time that it is unbelievable. Both of these martial artists were like mirror images. They complemented each other in so many different ways. Bruce was the yin and James was the yang, and together they comprised the whole of their existence. Bruce was always moving fast while James would have to keep Bruce's actions in check.

I believe that James was the only man Bruce would ever listen to on matters of great importance. This reflected on their martial arts training, business dealings, and matters of importance in their personal lives. Bruce would create the ideas for training equipment and James would build them. If one of them developed a more streamlined fighting technique, both of them would practice it until it could be performed flawlessly.

They were constantly challenging each other's wisdom in order to seek perfection in whatever they began.

Some of the valuable knowledge that I learned from these two great men is still practiced in my daily life. Bruce used to say, "Always adjust to the opponent but never become the opponent," or "Don't think. Thinking takes time, and while you are thinking, you'll get hit." Both he and James were constantly reminding me to "never concentrate on the essence of fighting, just react."

Perhaps the greatest philosophical lesson that James and Bruce taught me was to use humility instead of aggression and know when and when not to move. The principles of yin and yang are lessons that everyone can benefit from, and it has really helped me in my business and personal life.

The last time I saw James was at his birthday party that was held right before he passed on, and upon hearing of his demise, I was really shocked and it affected me very deeply. Six months later when I heard the news of Bruce in Hong Kong, I was struck again. It was like I had lost my father and one of my best friends.

Although Bruce and James are gone now, the spirit of their art will live on in the hearts of those who knew them well.

Hilton Wong

"Both James and Bruce were very proud men and it showed with the way they treated the children. Both of these men had physical talent, mental talent, and guts. They stood up for what they believed in, and it's very rare to find people like that these days."

The first time that I met James Lee was in the period prior to 1966 when James was teaching at the garage on Monticello Avenue in Oakland. I was studying judo at the time, and my brother Jim was already practicing Chinese gung-fu with James. Jim and myself would practice with each other and I became quite impressed with his technique and decided that I wanted to learn his art as well. It was through my brother's recommendation that I began training with James at his home in Oakland. Upon that first meeting I was quite impressed with the way that James taught the class. He was patient, a good instructor, and I liked the techniques that he was teaching.

During a period that lasted about three years, I would attend classes two days per week, each session for an hour to an hour and a half. In that time I really learned a lot from James and Bruce Lee. I could see that the techniques that James and Bruce were teaching were going through changes that were evolving from the traditional wing chun that I originally began learning. The techniques were becoming more simplified and cut down to save time when they were implemented. James was often introducing new training methods with the equipment that he was building so that we could reach higher plateaus of development. Most of the pads and punching equipment that James was using I had never seen used anywhere else before.

It was at James home where I first met Bruce Lee. He would train with James and with the students there at the garage. I was really impressed with Bruce's martial arts ability. Everybody talks about "lightning speed" in punching techniques but I didn't know the definition of lightning speed until I worked out with Bruce.

When he would move it were like somebody turned the light switch on and then off... just like that! There was nothing that you could do about it. After those sessions I finally knew the definition of lightning speed.

I recall times when I used to hold the punching pads for Bruce when he would perform his kicking techniques. They were extremely fast and above all powerful. It felt just like being hit by a truck. Every time that he would make one of those side-kicks I would fly backward about ten feet; I mean I would literally fly backward. I learned quite a bit from James and Bruce in addition to the martial arts that they were teaching. Both James and Bruce were honest and truthful and if they knew that you were honest and truthful, they would do anything to help you out. They had a mutual respect for each other and their students and I think of James as a father and Bruce as a brother. That's the way it was with those two guys.

The only thing that I noticed that ever frustrated James was when people would talk negatively about Bruce. Some people thought that Bruce was moving too fast and changing the classical styles of Chinese gung-fu to suit his own needs. James would get upset when people talked this way about Bruce. Both James and Bruce were very proud men and it showed with the way they treated the children. Both of these men had physical talent, mental talent, and guts. They stood up for what they believed in, and it's very rare to find people like that these days.

When I found out that James was sick, I asked him what his chances were for recovery and he said "about 50/50." During those times I would visit him quite often and when he died it shocked me very deeply. I could see the real "fighting spirit" in James all the way to the end.

When I had heard that Bruce had died about eight months later I couldn't believe it. There were so many times that I had heard that Bruce had got beat up or killed by a karate expert or something like that, so I naturally assumed that it was just another rumor. When I really found out that it was true, I couldn't believe it. In fact, it's still hard to accept even today. Those men had physical talent, mental talent, and guts.

Wally Jay

"The yin and yang combination of Jimmy and Bruce made them both compatible. They were the perfect complement of the other."

I first met James Lee at a martial arts exhibition in Oakland, California, in 1959. From that point, we performed together at many San Francisco Chinatown functions and soon after became very good friends.

My relationship with James grew immensely as I became acquainted with his versatile martial art skills. On many occasions, I visited his training site at Professor T.Y. Wong's gung-fu school (kwoon) in San Francisco Chinatown. Jimmy was a very serious student who utilized his workout time to the maximum. I held a great admiration for his martial arts skills. He was very knowledgeable of many aspects of martial arts techniques.

Jimmy was the first person that I have known who referred to the Chinese art of gung-fu as "kung fu." He informed me that "kung fu" sounded better and that was the way that it was pronounced in some of the Chinese dialects.

On many of the occasions that we performed together, Jimmy would perform incredible breaking feats. Since Jimmy was a performer of martial arts, I suppose that was one of the first things that we had in common. I had assembled a martial arts performing group by the name of "The Jay Follies, Jujitsu in Jest," and during the World War II years, we had performed for thousands of servicemen. The group was very popular even into the early 1960s.

It was during that period that Jimmy and myself became really acquainted with each other on a close and personal level.

As the founder and head instructor of the Island Judo Jujitsu Club, I sponsored two benefit luaus [Hawai'ian feasts] a year from 1957 to 1972.

On two of those occasions, Jimmy Lee was featured and demonstrated his fantastic breaking skills. Since many of our guests were martial artists, they were very impressed with his knowledge of these breaking techniques. One of the things that impressed many of the martial artists who attended the luaus was that Jimmy did not have any calluses on his hands whereas most martial artists who performed breaking feats had many calluses. The Hawai'ians were surprised to find that Jimmy's hands were unscarred. I later discovered that he took very good care of his hands after practicing breaking techniques by applying the Chinese herbal medicine known as "Yok Chalo."

I will never forget the time that he performed and broke five house bricks. He received a great round of applause. Then he piled three bricks on top of one another and proclaimed that he would break only the middle one without breaking the outer two. He commenced to center his focus energy at the pile and then struck the stack very sharply. He broke only the center brick. The audience of more than 1,000 spectators gave him a thundering round of applause.

He had performed a feat that very few martial artists have ever accomplished. The ability to control the strength and force of the penetrating strike is one of the most difficult of all breaking feats.

Several of my students and close associates began to train in the art of Chinese gung-fu with Jimmy.

I must mention that Jimmy never accepted remuneration for his breaking services even though he would spend a considerable amount of time, effort, and money to supply the bricks and boards. His humanitarian services are still remembered to this day.

Jimmy used to tell me that he was very proud of my achievements as a judo coach because the school had won many national and international competitive judo tournaments. It was during this phase of his martial arts career that he began writing books and asked my permission to publicize my achievements in his books. I graciously accepted and was honored for the privilege.

It was in 1962, three years after I had initially met Jimmy, that I had the opportunity to meet Bruce Lee. At the time, I was involved with taking a judo team to the Pacific Northwest. After we had competed and defeated the Obukan Judo Club of Portland, Oregon, it was at the advice of one of my judo student's parents, by the name of Dr. Jane Lee, that I come see a Chinese gentleman who was very good in the art of Chinese gung-fu. It was at that time that I discovered that Dr. Jane Lee had learned the cha-cha from Bruce Lee when he was originally in the Oakland and San Francisco area.

My first meeting occurred in the basement of a Chinese church in Seattle, Washington. It was there that Bruce was teaching a class in wing chun gung-fu. During our visit, I could see that this young man of about 22 years old was extremely proficient in the art of gung-fu. By that time, I had had plenty of meetings with martial arts masters of various styles but I had never met someone who was so skillful and proficient at the art of gung-fu. Not only was he skillful, he was very practical in his approach to self-defense.

Although Bruce was only half my age at the time, I became a believer in this young man's way of thinking about the fighting arts. During that initial visit, my judo team was in attendance and Bruce appreciated their competitive abilities. I mentioned to Bruce that we had several more tournaments to attend while in the area and he became interested in knowing the results as these events concluded.

The team attended the competition at the Vancouver Judo Club, and our junior and intermediate teams won overwhelmingly at the event. I called Bruce and he was really pleased to know the results and that we had won. Then it was on to the Randori School of Judo in Portland, Oregon, where we won all of the matches. Again, I called Bruce to let him know the results and he became excited and said again how pleased he was of the results. He also mentioned that he was really impressed with the strength and technique of my judo players. It was at that point that I knew that Bruce took a serious interest in all forms of martial arts training.

When I returned to my school in Alameda, I immediately called Jimmy Lee and explained that I had met an exceptional Chinese man by the name of Bruce Lee who was teaching wing chun in the Seattle area. This is when I learned that Jimmy had already heard of this gentleman and was familiar with him through a previous meeting that Jimmy's brother had had on a prior trip to the San Francisco area. I gave Jimmy the address of Bruce and within two weeks, Bruce was visiting with James at his home on Monticello Avenue in Oakland, California. I recalled Bruce telephoning me from Oakland and wanting me to visit him at James' home. I went and together we discussed the martial arts for several hours. This was the first of many such personal visits that occurred while Bruce was living at James' home for the next three years.

In that period, both Jimmy and Bruce became regular visitors to my school in Alameda. During these visits we would talk and discuss martial arts theory, application, and general topics of related interest. Our meetings were of mutual benefit in many ways.

We would exchange techniques and practical solutions to complex fighting strategies. I admired Bruce's lightning speed and awesome punching power. In addition, he was incredibly proficient in the wing chun chi sao (sticking hands) close-range techniques. His vast knowledge and the ability to apply it to self-defense situations were uncanny. In some of the visitation sessions, he would toy with us while applying some of his unique hand combinations.

During those exchange encounters, Bruce and I became very close friends and were constantly exchanging new ideas on old martial arts principles. I could sense that sometime in the future he would be doing great things in the martial arts world.

It was during Bruce's Oakland Years that I had the opportunity to meet Linda. She and Bruce visited my home while living in the Bay Area. I believe that she had been a student of Bruce's for about six months when Bruce asked her to demonstrate her punching and kicking techniques to me. She excelled admirably and I could see why Bruce was so proud of her.

During one of the first Island Judo Jujitsu Club's Hawai'ian luaus, Bruce and Jimmy performed a well-rounded martial arts demonstration. Jimmy would perform the breaking feats, Bruce would demonstrate his awesome punching power, they would practice wing chun self-defense techniques together, and finally close with an exhibition on the *mook jong* [wing chun practice dummy]. They were an incredible team to watch when they demonstrated their martial arts talents. The audience would get so excited when they were performing. At both times that Bruce performed at the benefit luaus for the club, Bruce refused to accept compensation for his services. He was like Jimmy in that regard and wanted the monies that I offered to go into the travel fund for the judo team.

During the latter part of the Oakland Years, Bruce was beginning to make inroads into Hollywood.

It was there where he had secured a role as "Kato" in *The Green Hornet* television series. When he and Linda finally moved to Hollywood, Bruce would continually stay in contact with me by telephone and letters to keep me updated on his projects.

I had the opportunity to visit their lovely home in Bel Air with several friends who were traveling with me. I fondly remember Bruce impressing my friends with his devastating kicking power. Most people who witnessed a small man of 135 pounds execute powerful kicking techniques that possessed the force of men twice his size were completely shocked by the force that Bruce could generate. He would execute seemingly short-range kicks to the large bag that was hung in his home, and the entire rafter structure of the house would shake. It was frightening to see such a display of awesome power. Bruce was very proud of his martial arts library, which included virtually every form of martial arts book that had ever been published. In his collection were many books on both Eastern and Western philosophy, boxing, French savate, judo, karate, and Chinese gung-fu of many styles.

He would show me books that were extremely rare collector's items. While on the visits to Bruce and Linda's home, we had the opportunity to discuss many of Bruce's future plans. Again, I sensed that this man was really moving in the direction of bigger and better things.

Bruce also related to me that he was very proud of his wife Linda and their child Brandon, who was a small child at the time. They meant so much to him. He was a very positive person in everything that he attempted. In our conversations, he would give details of his future plans in the movies and mention that one day he would have a beautiful home on a hill and hopefully become a millionaire sometime in the near future. I was not surprised at Bruce's success and I knew that he had so much knowledge to offer the world and he was destined to make improvements and open the eyes of martial artists all over the globe. While Bruce was still playing the part of "Kato," he would continually make trips back up to the Oakland area. On one of those trips he was our guest of honor at the city of Alameda's first judo invitational tournament. He really enjoyed the enthusiasm of the spectators and spent most of his time signing autographs for the fans who enjoyed his performances in *The Green Hornet.* He was really great with the fans and spectators alike.

I felt that there were times that Bruce was feeling insecure because of the fast-changing series of events that are always occurring in Hollywood, but he knew that he had the potential to change with the times. His goals were always beyond those of most people and he constantly strived to bring the best out of himself. The last time that I talked to Bruce by telephone, I knew that he was beginning to feel quite secure with the future that he had planned for himself and his family. He expressed more confidence than ever before. His assertiveness was beginning to show in the films that he was making in Hong Kong, and it was not long before the entire world was aware of this great man's talent.

During the Bruce Lee era, all martial arts schools profited by his exposure. People became martial arts conscious, and many unscrupulous instructors undoubtedly took advantage of the unsuspecting public.

The shock of Bruce Lee's death affected millions of his fans throughout the world. In many of my international visits and seminars, since they knew Bruce was a very dear personal friend of mine, they always ask, "What did Bruce die of?" He was a hero to them and they express concern for everything that this great man has done.

After Bruce's demise, Linda sent me a large photo of Bruce that is permanently displayed in my school. It is a picture that I cherish very much. Bruce left a lot of memories for me. They were very special memories. Linda is a very special person to me, and throughout the hardships that she has faced she has carried on very well. She is very strong and I hold a great admiration for her.

The fond memories that Bruce and Jimmy left with me will always be cherished. They have proved that they truly cared for me through their friendship and help. The yin and yang combination of Jimmy and Bruce made them both compatible. They were the perfect complement of the other. Jimmy always kept a low profile and he was one of the greatest assets to Bruce while Bruce was struggling for the stardom that he so justly deserved. Both of those men were ahead of their times.

Ed Parker

"It was James, however, who continued experimenting with Bruce and training equipment to develop a more substantial martial artist."

James Y. Lee was not only a good martial artist, but also a person whom I considered to be a close friend. We met often in the 1960s to discuss, analyze, delve, and experiment with the various systems he had learned. He was a rare individual who was not bound to Oriental traditions. Because of his willingness to keep an open mind, he developed innovative qualities that led to interesting and creative discussions. We continually shared our mutual interests and made it a standard policy to inform the other of any new or interesting developments. It was he who phoned me to tell me of his meeting an accomplished practitioner who also shared nontraditional views.

He told me that his newly acquired friend was at his home and invited me to fly to Oakland, California, that weekend to meet him. When I arrived at James' home it was Bruce Lee whom I was introduced to; James description and opinion of Bruce Lee were not exaggerated. Bruce Lee was indeed an accomplished practitioner. He popped the air when he punched, and his concepts were practical and realistic. James and I both recognized Bruce's potential and discussed ways to expose Bruce to the public. James felt that my contacts in Hollywood could launch Bruce to stardom. As I pursued this avenue I was able to aid Bruce in securing the role of

"Kato" in *The Green Hornet* series. The rest of Bruce's accomplishments are now history.

James Lee continued his close relationship with Bruce and I, exchanging martial arts concepts and principles. It was James, however, who continued experimenting with Bruce and training equipment to develop a more substantial and practical martial artist. Had death not overcome James and Bruce, their innovative efforts would have had a greater influence on the martial arts. While both of these superbly talented individuals are no longer with us, their influence still prevails.

Ralph Castro

"If it were not for many of the concepts of Bruce and James, the martial arts would never be where they are today."

It was ironic that Ed Parker and I were visiting Chinatown in San Francisco when we noticed a book titled *Fighting Arts of the Orient: Elemental Karate and Kung-Fu* that was displayed in the window of one of the small shops there. Upon further investigation, and since

we were both actively involved with the study of martial arts, we discovered that the book was written by a gentleman by the name of James Yimm Lee, who lived across the bay in Oakland, California. As I recall, this was in 1960 or the earlier part of 1961 when very little was written regarding the martial arts, and our curiosity was whetted to the point where we wanted to meet the author of this book. Essentially, we wanted to find out what other martial arts practitioners had to offer and decided to seek this gentleman out.

Ed and myself called, made an appointment, and visited James Lee immediately after discovering his address. This first meeting was rewarding in many ways, and little did we know that it would be the beginning of a long and lasting friendship. James was a very nice guy and extremely easy to get along with and was very open-minded in sharing his style of martial arts. This was a time when most styles of Oriental martial arts were so secretive that very few people had access to this knowledge outside of the elders that had studied in the Orient.

He was a very sincere and honest person who was not only interested in the martial arts but was willing to share and exchange ideas with other people. From that early beginning, it was James that opened the doors to many of the secretive and little-known styles taught in the secluded areas of San Francisco Chinatown to both Ed and myself.

We became very good friends with many of the instructors in

the inner circles and on many occasions, through the introductions by Jimmy, we were fortunate to visit the annual events held by the martial artists in those inner circles. Jimmy was well known and respected by the elderly martial arts masters, and his introductions were well received by these masters. On occasion, I had the opportunity to watch him work out and was truly impressed with his martial arts skills. He was knowledgeable of many forms of movement and a wide variety of techniques.

I discovered that the way that Jimmy got his reputation was that when he wanted to learn something new he would go where it was possible in order to learn, with no reservations toward the style or method taught by others. He had a lot of rare knowledge and martial information but was always searching for new ways and types of martial arts techniques. He could do this without making a pest of himself and was well liked by everyone who knew him.

I recall James being a real showman when he performed his unique iron-palm breaking techniques at one of Wally Jay's luaus. Jimmy was incredible at breaking bricks and boards and would often make jokes about his ability. During one of these instances when he had selected one brick out of a large stack that he would attempt to break, when it did not break, but the whole stack was demolished, he laughed and said that he "didn't do it right." The audience would really watch in dismay and then applaud that they would all be broken. Jimmy was a real artist at breaking, and he knew the entire science of this rare subject. He knew the proper power, timing, sensitivity control, and right amount of pressure required to break a certain brick within a given stack. Many people used to use spacers and such to increase the number of bricks or boards that they could break, but Jimmy never did it that way. He relied on his real knowledge of power and speed. Jimmy was one of the very few people I have ever seen who could break a large stack of unspaced bricks with the back of the hand. In fact, up until the time that I saw him perform this feat I had never seen anyone else perform this type of breaking.

Even now, there are just a few who I have seen duplicate this display of pure power. His hands were extremely conditioned without the slightest signs of calluses. He gave me some of the iron-palm medicine that he used, and I still have some of it to this day.

In the many meetings that James and I have had over the years, I was always impressed with his thirst for knowledge and wanting to find a better way of doing everything. I think that is why he was so dedicated to the martial arts profession.

We would constantly shuttle between his home, my home, and Chinatown for meetings and just to talk about martial arts. It was one topic that we shared and could always relate to when we were together. I think our mutual interest in the subject was the cohesion that drew us so close together.

It was through Jimmy that I first met Bruce Lee. As I recall, it was a weekend when Ed Parker was visiting me from Los Angeles, and suddenly I received a call from Jimmy who was at the other end of the line and he said, "You have to get over here and see this guy named Bruce Lee. He's fantastic." So immediately, Ed and myself paid a visit to Jimmy's home on Monticello. When we first met, both Ed and myself could sense by watching some of his speed and power techniques that he was incredibly fantastic and had a firm grasp of the martial arts. It was immediately after that that we visited my studio in San Francisco, where further exchanges of ideas and techniques took place. Bruce was an abundance of energy and was always very active and loved to display his martial arts ability. Pound for pound, he was a very impressive person. Bruce only weighed about 140 pounds at the time and was extremely fast and possessed an incredible amount of power. It was then that Ed and myself knew what James was talking about. In remembering those early days, I recall Bruce wanting to demonstrate his back knuckle strike and he asked me to block it. I was assuming that he had been very successful with it in previous demonstrations and wanted to accommodate his intentions.

Bruce performed this with me but I did not do the type of blocking technique that he expected but instead I executed a back knuckle strike myself, which neutralized his strike while redirecting my energy in his direction. Bruce was surprised and said, "You son-of-a-gun . . . that's the first time that that has ever happened." I told Bruce that I couldn't do things his way but had to do it my way. From that point on we hit it off really good. He was a very understanding man who was intelligent and possessed an analytical mind. These early meetings began during 1961 or the earlier part of 1962 and were the beginning of another close and dear friendship.

On many occasions, Jimmy, Bruce, and myself would get together at my home or at James' house or at a Chinese restaurant in Chinatown and discuss martial arts. I suppose we were all talking shop and enjoying each other's company so much that most other subjects did not matter. We became the best of friends in life as well as martial arts and it was always a real pleasure to see Bruce and James.

Some of those fond recollections are always great to recall. Bruce was a real practical joker as well as a great joke teller. He used to always say that the Chinese appreciated what they read whereas the Americans never really appreciated what they were reading. Then he would ask if anyone knew why this was so. When someone would ask him why, he would reply, "Because when the Chinese read, they read up and down so their head showed the gesture that they appreciated what they were reading, and the Americans were always reading from left to right so they must not appreciate what they were reading." Everyone would laugh when Bruce pulled that one on a nonsuspecting person.

When we would visit or plan to meet at different restaurants in San Francisco or Oakland, Bruce would arrive early, hide behind a door or panel wall, and wait for us to arrive. When we would enter, Bruce would quickly and surprisingly jump out and execute some martial arts techniques while making sudden yells *(kiai)*. After several of those antics, we would always expect that from Bruce. He was great at pulling those kinds of practical jokes.

Another fond memory that I have of Bruce was at a time after he had become famous as "Kato" in *The Green Hornet.* On this particular week he was visiting in the Bay Area and came over to my home to spend the day. I asked Bruce if he would mind picking up my children at the Catholic school that they were attending. Bruce had that gleam in his eyes as he grabbed the keys and took off for the door. Upon arriving at the school, he approached the Sister in charge of the classes and said that he was there to pick up April, May, June, July, and Boss Castro.

As Bruce entered the classrooms, all of the children in the entire class instantly recognized him as "Kato" and began to cause a real commotion in the class. The teachers were not too pleased with the disruption, but all of the students were very excited. My children had mentioned on several occasions that they knew Bruce Lee but many of the children disbelieved it until that day. After that, there was a different type of respect for my children by the other students. When Bruce brought the children home and told me that story, he was just as excited as the children. He really loved the children.

Bruce was constantly updating his martial arts demonstrations to give a clearer perspective of the essential elements of self-defense to the audiences that he performed for. His ability to demonstrate the one- and three-inch punches and the innovative ways that he performed full-contact sparring with the body armor woke many people up to the real and practical side of the martial arts. I would have to credit him for introducing the real full-contact arts to the United States.

If it were not for many of the concepts of Bruce and James, the martial arts would never be where they are today. Bruce was one of the first to excel in complete body conditioning for all-out fighting in martial arts practice, and I think all of the progressive martial artists learned quite a lesson from him in that respect.

In eulogy, there are many things that can be said for both of those true warriors. In reflecting on why Bruce and James got along so well, I would have to say that they really spoke their minds and had a very strong respect for each other.

Even though Bruce was the teacher and James was the student, they were friends both in and out of the class environment. As James became an instructor of the jeet kune do concepts, he became very relaxed and easygoing but was stern when it was needed, whereas Bruce was always direct. This reflected the dissimilarities in their teaching style, but one was a part of the other. Both men were setting goals for themselves that made them reach higher and farther than most people would ever attempt.

I know that Bruce was just beginning to reach his goals at the time of his demise. He wanted to take the martial arts into the realm of motion pictures so that the entire world would become familiar with its existence. In retrospect, after thinking of those earlier years, I really knew that Bruce would reach those goals. He got the chance and made the words gung-fu and Bruce Lee household names.

When James became quite ill, I never really knew it. He was a true warrior in the spirit. The last time that I spoke to him was at Wally's luau in 1972 and he was just his good-natured self. Shortly after, it came as a stunning surprise when I heard that he passed away. I lost a close and dear friend.

James Yimm Lee is the epitome of a true warrior and was always loyal, dedicated, and had an open mind. Bruce was a scholar as well as a true warrior who possessed a rare combination of honor and dignity. Together these men were inseparable in the true spirit of martial arts. Jimmy and Bruce have had lasting effects on my emotions, and I have always treasured their friendship.

I can still picture them even today as if I was waiting for them to call and say, "Hey, come on down and let's go to Chinatown." My thought of James' departure was that although he is no longer here physically, he is with Bruce and me in the spirit; and when Bruce departed, I thought to myself, well, they are together in the spirit and we are separated by the great beyond. Some day, I'm going to go their route and when I do, we are going to meet again. They were first but eventually we will be together again.

Bruce Lee and James Lee will always be very close friends to my family and myself and we will never forget them, physically or in the spirit.

Dan Inosanto

"James Lee was definitely Bruce Lee's sounding board, punching bag, and training partner, but above all one of Bruce's closest friends."

James Lee was a man I truly admired and respected. My first contact with James Lee was long before I met Bruce Lee. In fact, though I met him in 1961, I read his book in 1959 entitled *Fighting Arts of the Orient*. This little book, which numbers about 54 pages, is still considered one of the finest, most informative books on the martial arts. Very little is known of James Lee because he was under the shadow of Bruce Lee, but to me, James Lee in his own right was an outstanding martial arts practitioner, teacher, and writer on the martial arts. In fact, it was James who prodded Bruce into writing his first book, *Chinese Gung-Fu: The Philosophical Art of Self-Defense*. James, besides running the Oakland Jun Fan Gung Fu Institute for Bruce Lee, was very instrumental in creating much of the training equipment that was to be used in the jeet kune do training.

Many people thought of James as a physical person only, but *Fighting Arts of the Orient* and *Modern Kung-Fu Karate* were just some of the books he wrote to display his intellectual ability to express himself.

As for Bruce Lee's conditioning, it was in this area that Bruce perhaps picked up a few tricks from James. James Lee had been a champion weightlifter and gymnast in his youth. I think credit should be given James for getting Bruce interested in developing his body. I

don't think Bruce started serious weight training until after he met James. Even though Bruce's system was based on elusiveness and speed, he still highly believed that you had to have great strength. In fact, because of James, he used to overtrain in this area.

Because James was a welder by trade, Bruce made him responsible for turning out many of the mechanical training devices that Bruce used to develop his amazing power and force. The original *Mon Fat Jong* [thousand-way dummy] that James created for kicking and various hand techniques for Bruce was ingenious.

This ingenious device with car springs and shock absorbers causes a human-like effect when you kick it and was probably responsible for developing Bruce's side-kick to a high degree. His foot obstruction and shin-kick apparatus also shows the genius of James Lee. He also developed Bruce's neck and headlock apparatus.

One of my favorite sayings from James was, "Any knowledge or implement when used without moral conscience can be a force for destruction. This is equally true whether it is physical or atomic power. If mayhem is the sadistic desire of anyone who takes up fighting arts of the Orient, I really think it is much easier to get an axe, hammer, or pistol. Why spend weeks, months, and even years to develop the skill and power to hurt someone? Don't be overconfident, thinking that no one but you has this knowledge. What one man has achieved, another can certainly exceed, whether it is in wisdom, wealth, or strength. Every man we meet is superior to us in some way."

James Lee was definitely Bruce Lee's sounding board, punching bag, and training partner, but above all one of Bruce's closest friends. It gives me great honor to write this portion of the book for James Lee, my *Sihing* [senior] in jeet kune do.

Sam Allred

"Bruce was equipped with a radiant nature, great vitality, and a keen and eager mind and was willing to extend its knowledge to the utmost limits."

I had known Bruce for many years. This originally stemmed from our mutual interest in the martial arts. Our visits and many meetings would usually occur before, during, or after various karate-related activities.

Upon his demise I was asked by *Black Belt* magazine to write his official biography. My work on the biography consisted mainly of interviews with Bruce's better-known students and close friends. These included Steve McQueen, James Coburn, John Saxon, and Stirling Silliphant, but also included many of his martial arts friends such as Chuck Norris, Bob Wall, and Wally Jay, among others.

By the time the book was published, I was very likely as knowledgeable about Bruce as anyone. I had re-formed some of my own opinions of Bruce through the extensive time spent studying him

through the contact with so many who knew him so well. I will try to describe the Bruce Lee that I knew and came to know!

Bruce eagerly rushed out to greet life in its many facets. He was equipped with a radiant nature, great vitality, and a keen and eager mind and was willing to extend its knowledge to the utmost limits. Knowledge of those things that interested him most was always sacred and reflected in his action and deeds.

Wit, cleverness, and intelligence were among his gifts, as were charm and a great ability to be entertaining. For many of those relatively few people who possess such traits, the danger is to coast through life on wit and personality. Bruce was capable of winning people over simply by appearing on the scene. But for Bruce, the creative urge was too powerful to permit coasting. He had to leave the world better than he had found it ... and he had to shine.

He was aimed toward success throughout his life and could have hardly been unsuccessful. He made profound mental and physical growth a lifetime task and was still impatient with his accomplishments, knowing the shortness of life. His genius required self-betterment and self-sacrifice, and his ego made him pursue greatness to lofty heights. His inner drive and sense of self-worth amounted almost to a neurosis, which he usually dealt with constructively. A certain power and authority, which amounted almost to pompousness, was evident in his speech. He didn't merely say things ... he stated them, and this had its effect on his listeners.

Bruce had an extremely complex emotional nature subject to discontent and depression. His powers of observation were acute and among his strong abilities was the ability to learn from experience. He was not all-trusting.

He could outguess most people and had a sixth sense that told him things most people would miss. He was usually not outwardly noticeable. He was a first-class critic, seeing through phoniness and pretensions.

Bruce craved admiration, excitement, and adulation and he channeled these needs into his charisma. This turned out to be an excellent aspect for dealing with the tremendous numbers of people looking for a "Bruce Lee." His charisma and magnetism nearly became tangible . . . as we all know.

Jon Lee

"When I think of James, my younger brother, I see a raging bull!"

When I think of James, my younger brother, I see a raging bull! He was very quick-tempered, and he was not afraid to take on anyone who got in his way.

I think back to the time when all three of us brothers were quite young. Whenever my mother was out visiting friends and father was at work, inevitably, James would get into a fight. It was then that our sisters would usually have to call Mother to come home to stop the fighting.

It was not uncommon for chairs to be broken, doors smashed down, and other types of disarrangement with the household furniture. James had a bad habit of throwing things and breaking them.

It came as no surprise to me that when he grew up, he gravitated toward all types of physical sports. His main interests were in swimming, wrestling, and weightlifting. It was later that he developed an interest in gung-fu and all types of martial arts.

In his personal life, James was a very carefree sort of person and basically an extrovert at heart. He had an uncanny nature to make friends quite easily with total strangers.

I do not think that James was the type of person who liked to be alone and spend quiet moments in meditation. Ever since I can remember, he liked to surround himself with friends.

In his adult years, he enjoyed "nightclubbing" with his close friends and associates. In fact, I was never surprised when he brought home friends and they would stay until the early hours socializing and enjoying themselves.

He was a person who lived for the present and there were no long-range plans for his life.

Financially, James had very little regard for future spending. To him, money was for spending and there was no need to save it for a rainy day. He spent money for fun and pleasure on his friends and close acquaintances. It was not unusual for him to loan considerable sums of money to friends and never expect it to be repaid. In all likelihood, much of those loans were never repaid but that was the way James felt about money.

Although James was not a college graduate and scored rather low in his high school curriculum, he was very well read on many topics. He was extremely knowledgeable of current events.

James studied the Chinese language for several years and became quite adept at reading, speaking, and writing the language. One of his favorite ways of speaking to the Chinese people was to quote some of the ancient Chinese proverbs while watching the reactions from his listeners. He thought that this was great fun.

His real strong point was in the friendliness that he showed friends and strangers alike. He could put a person at ease from the first moment they met and had a knack for drawing out the other person and making him or her feel comfortable and talkative.

He was always lending a helping hand to others who were less fortunate, even to the point that some of his associates took advantage of his generosity.

His philosophy was that the future would take care of itself, and therefore, why should he worry about such mundane matters.

James was the strongest of the three of us and participated in physical activities that required a great deal of strength and endurance. Who could have ever guessed that he would be the one who succumbed to a fatal disease at such a young age? There is an old Chinese proverb, which accurately describes his life: "Human fortunes are as unpredictable as the weather."

Karena Beverly Lee

"Whenever times got tough for my dad, Uncle Bruce would help him through it by telling him, 'You are a fighter! Consider the odds, hang in there, and keep blasting!'"

A Tribute to Two Great Men

Some people enter our lives and quickly leave; others stay for a while, leaving footprints on our hearts. Bruce Lee is one of those very special personalities who have remained unforgettable to myself and all who knew him. He has left an indelible imprint on our lives. Millions of fans around the world, who still idolize him ten years now after his death, have made him an immortal legend in our time.

Much has been told about the great achievements made by this man, but little mention has been made of the earlier years in his struggle to the top. This is where my father, the late James Yimm Lee, played a very important role in helping the young man from Hong Kong get his start in this country and making Bruce's dreams for the spread of gung-fu a reality. It is with fond memories that I reminisce about the "good old days" from 1962 to 1965 when the then-unknown Bruce Lee and his wife, Linda, lived with my family for those three years in Oakland, California.

The friendship that developed between Bruce Lee and my dad was an unusually close one; they became like brothers and knew each other very well. My brother, Greglon, and I always called him "Uncle" Bruce. Dad had not only gained the best comrade he had ever had in his life; but we as children received something precious too—namely, a confidant who had lot of influence upon us as we were growing up.

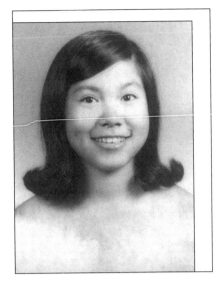

Upon first meeting Bruce in 1959, my father had the honor of becoming Bruce Lee's very first pupil in gung-fu. My father was twenty years older than Bruce and already had a rather broad background in physical conditioning and various types of martial arts. Yet this younger man was to become Dad's Sifu or master instructor and Dad his devoted follower. In the short initial period of time that Dad sparred with Bruce, he learned more than in all of his previous years of training. Bruce was the only instructor Dad had ever met who could actually defend against any kind of attack without having the situation prearranged. Dad had quit his prior study of useless forms in the classical style in disgust; now along came Bruce, who rekindled his enthusiasm for the martial arts. Dad was amazed by the young man's remarkable speed and strength and really appreciated the simple, direct, practical applications in his unique fighting style.

Dad always considered it a great privilege to be able to study under Uncle Bruce and became his assistant instructor. While in daily contact living together in Oakland, both men benefited from each other's companionship. James Lee, who for years had been "crammed and distorted by the classical mess," now became more efficient in self-defense. Bruce's techniques emphasized simplicity of the art—smooth, short, and fast. They were stripped down to their essential purpose without any wasted motions. Under Bruce Lee's philosophical training, Dad's outlook and attitude on life changed too. Dad seemed to have turned over a new leaf and became interested in health foods and natural foods and vitamins. He even began jogging. It was the most creative period in his life; he grew mentally, spiritually, and physically. From his circle of gung-fu practitioners, James Lee gained many new friends. They would enjoy chatting with him in our living room on various subjects like current events or their hobbies and other activities other than just gung-fu. Many would do favors and render their professional services to both Dad and Bruce.

Uncle Bruce would usually plan surprise birthday parties for Dad and invite many of his gung-fu students, even later on when Bruce and Linda moved to Los Angeles for Uncle Bruce's television career. Dad's genius is shown by his invention of numerous gung-fu training devices and apparatus during this time. The success of his books on martial arts such as *Wing Chun Kung Fu*, his home mail-order business, and continual public interest in his jeet kune do gung-fu classes—all helped James Lee gain quite a reputation in the martial arts world and gave him a greater sense of accomplishment in life. Furthermore, Bruce Lee blossomed too in these Oakland Years during which my father helped the future superstar reach his full potential. Dad was most generous in offering Uncle Bruce and Linda a free place to stay so the master could concentrate on perfecting his art and not have to worry about earning a regular income for a while. Dad, who had broken records in weight training and bodybuilding, passed his expertise along to Bruce so he could develop the well-known, much admired he-man physique.

A welder by trade, Dad designed and constructed many ingenious gung-fu training devices for Uncle Bruce, which were of immeasurable value in quickening his lightning-fast reflexes or increasing his strength and power. Dad, who was already experienced as an author, aided Bruce in his first literary attempt of writing and publishing his first book on the martial arts. Exhibitions and tournaments that they performed in did much to expose Bruce Lee to the public eye. The two men opened a Jun Fan Kung Fu School, which Uncle Bruce used to refer to as the "James Lee Oakland kwoon." Small groups of students were chosen on the basis of character and potential. Until that time, the secret art of self-defense had been kept pretty much among the Asian people only; Westerners knew very little about it. These two men were among the first to accept students from all races and backgrounds, which caused a martial arts movement that not only swept the country but also spread throughout the world.

Neither man's aim was purely materialistic; they never commercialized the school nor advertised publicly. Yet they got eager students as well as some outside challengers. Uncle Bruce was more concerned with the quality of his art and sought constant improvement. He used to analyze home movies of boxing championship matches and browse through used bookstores to find old books on the various fighting arts. By daily study he learned all he could and developed his own best style. Dad was always a willing partner with whom Bruce could develop new techniques. It was with such hard work and total dedication that his creativity flourished while in Oakland and surely this period of his life was instrumental in making Bruce Lee the best in his field.

It gave him some roots from which he later branched out to reach greater plateaus.

My memories of Bruce Lee go deeper than just the invincible

killer image that is portrayed across the silver screen. That is but a glimpse of the uniqueness of his personality. The tremendous intellectual philosophy, which he applied not only to his art but also to life in general, stands out in my mind. Mental gung-fu was always coming at you, not just the physical show. The real Bruce Lee was a man who could sit meditatively and reflect thus:

> Be like water making its way through cracks. Do not be assertive, but adjusting ourselves to the object, we shall find the way around or through it. The softer [more pliable] a substance is, the narrower the crack through which it may pass. ... If nothing within you stays rigid, outward things will disclose themselves. Moving, be like water. Still, be like a mirror. Respond like an echo. ... Nothingness cannot be defined; the softest thing cannot be snapped.

Uncle Bruce had a vocabulary that could surpass most Americans. He used to teach me the meanings of uncommon words. He had a huge, ever-growing personal library of thousands of volumes that covered many subjects. He spent many happy hours reciting beloved poetic passages from great works of literature.

I owe my own love of books and learning in part to the fine example Bruce set as a serious scholar and deep thinker. He believed a man at peace with himself could be at peace with others. He was a dynamic speaker with a keen sense of humor, which added to his charisma, or power of his being the center of attention. Being around Uncle Bruce made my adolescence more interesting and happier.

He was always a very inspiring person who encouraged me to keep striving. His last words to me were, "Keep up the good work." Whenever times got tough for my dad, Uncle Bruce would help him through it by telling him, "You are a fighter! Consider the odds, hang in there, and keep blasting!" I try to keep on growing in all aspects of my life.

There is a photograph of Dad working out with Uncle Bruce that I have treasured over the years; it is autographed with the following inscription:

> To my comrade James Lee—We are always in the process of becoming and NOTHING is fixed. Have no rigid system in you and you will be flexible to change with the ever changing.
>
> OPEN yourself and flow at once with the TOTAL flowing now.
>
> PEACE, LOVE, BROTHERHOOD
>
> Bruce

When Bruce and Linda moved away, Bruce always kept us up to date with his work; as offers to him were getting better, we sensed that he was bound to hit the big time. Dad used to say that "Bruce was born under a lucky star; he happened to be at the right place at the right time." There was lots of organized planning along the way and Uncle Bruce never moved before the course was well charted. Uncle Bruce was a maker of his own destiny, or as he used to claim, "Circumstances, hell, I make circumstances." He possessed a wide variety of talents; it is rare today to find a man with such a winning combination. Like a real diamond, it is hard to imitate and impossible to replace.

Bruce felt that he would not live a very long life, and somehow inside he knew his destiny and felt the clock ticking away. This may be why he was always pushing himself so hard to achieve the many accomplishments done in so short a period of time. It may also be why he hoped to retire at an early age and go into quiet seclusion like a Taoist priest, to devote himself wholeheartedly to internal nourishment.

With his external gung-fu art at a state of perfection, he could then concentrate on developing his inner nature. With completion of this training of about ten years he would come out again to serve his fellow men, to contribute to society and this world again. Unfortunately he died too soon and could not fulfill this dream. This is a loss to us all.

Though Bruce Lee's years of life only number 32, it was a meaningful period that left quite an impact on the world. Neither Bruce nor my dad probably ever realized the impact and force that their gung-fu was to have on the martial arts world. When Uncle Bruce was just starting out in Hollywood as "Kato" in *The Green Hornet* television series, he chose me to be the president of his fan club. Later that task was turned over to professionals at the studios. It would have been very difficult, if not impossible, to handle all of the fan mail and to keep up with all of the publicity from all of the foreign presses that was continually coming out.

As of the more recent past, Mr. Norman Borine conducted much of this work with the "World of Bruce Lee" museum in Los Angeles, California.

My father and Bruce Lee showed me that patience, persistence, and determination are omnipotent in fulfilling your dreams and attaining success. Both men worked hard and gained the respect of their families, friends, and followers. Their efforts helped raise the image of all Asian people, which would in turn help to promote harmony and understanding between East and West. Although they are now gone, they are not forgotten....

"Parting"

Who knows when meeting shall ever be? It might be for years, or it might be forever. Let us then take a lump of clay, wet it, pat it, and make an image of you, and an image of me. Then smash them, crash them, and, with a little water, knead them together. And out of the clay we'll remake an image of you, and an image of me. Thus in my clay, there's a little of you, and in your clay, there's a little of me. And nothing will ever set us apart. Living, we'll be forever in each other's heart, and dead, we'll be buried together.

By Bruce Lee

I know their memory will live on.
BRUCE & JAMES
As remembered by friends…

Greglon Yimm Lee

"Bruce and my dad. … They were warriors, philosophers, technicians, artists, writers, and hard workers who dedicated themselves to elevating their knowledge by seeking a path that had not been traveled at the time."

Although I was quite young when my father and Bruce Lee became close personal friends, there are many vivid recollections of their association while Bruce and Linda lived at our home on Monticello Avenue in Oakland.

In remembering my father, I should mention at the outset of this eulogy that I miss my father and Bruce more than ever. My father was a man who thought of others and always tried to help friends who were in need. He did not get caught up in the superficial aspects of life. He sought a simple path that led him through many creative avenues. It was his belief that hard work and determination could accomplish anything that anyone ever wanted. I believe that his creativity stemmed from his ever-changing ideas to make things better by becoming simpler in the practical sense. He and Bruce were almost identical in this way of thinking. My father was never afraid to change his ideas for the purpose of improving them. As I recall, he never followed ritualism or tradition for its own sake. From this point of view, he did not wait for others to initiate, but chose to be a self-starter. Both he and Bruce were constantly initiating projects that were challenging, to say the least. I honestly believe that they were years ahead of their time in creativity and development in martial arts concepts. It is easy to see why the concepts of jeet kune do are still as relevant today as they were in the Oakland Years.

Even today, I do not completely understand all of the concepts that they formulated in my youth, but I have grown to appreciate the wisdom and ideals that they set for themselves.

Many people may never really know the depth and width of the knowledge that emerged from the meeting of these two men, since it is virtually impossible to convey feeling in words or pictures. But I do know that their understanding of life, for the short period of time that they spent in this world, was obvious to everyone who came in contact with them.

It was very obvious to me that my father and Bruce had a great mutual respect for one another. The way that they tackled martial arts projects together while training and developing was reflected in their books, equipment, writings, and teachings that have been left behind for future generations, and indicates at least in part, some of this respect.

They were serious without taking life too seriously. They were so similar yet so different. If the yin and yang were ever meant to complement the other in an interacting fashion, it certainly was reflected in the interactions of Bruce and my father.

They were warriors, philosophers, technicians, artists, writers, and hard workers who dedicated themselves to elevating their knowledge by seeking a path that had not been traveled at the time. It was also a real privilege to have Bruce and Linda live in our home and take care of us in our childhood. There are many memorable experiences that will never be forgotten. Linda was always there helping and encouraging my sister and me, and it was really wonderful to have such guidance. I will always be indebted for the kindness shown to us at that young age.

Bruce taught me to be myself and not to copy others but learn to be the best you can, and to keep trying and striving for what you want to accomplish. He taught me to be my own judge and to always recognize your strengths and weaknesses and to do what was best for different situations. My mental awareness and ways of thinking have been influenced tremendously by Bruce's early teachings. Bruce and my father inspired me to use my natural talents to the best of my abilities and to never be afraid to make changes.

I fondly recall many of the times that Bruce and my father would take great pleasure in joking and laughing at themselves when things did not go as planned. This really showed me the lighter sides of their personalities.

I am thankful for having such a unique father and a friend such as Bruce Lee, and as the years pass since their demise, I become even more aware of the influence that they had on my life. They will always be missed in both my heart and mind.

Bryant Wong

"James was very popular with most of the people of Oakland Chinatown and most knew him as the "Mayor of Chinatown" because of his outgoing and friendly personality."

I first met James Lee at Washington Park Beach in Alameda, California. In those days, the Alameda beach was like muscle beach and all of the bodybuilders would gather there on the weekends. We were automatically attracted to each other since we were both involved in bodybuilding. It was not long after our first meeting that we began to train regularly at many of the gyms in the Oakland area.

James was a serious bodybuilder who trained hard and did not mess around when it came to training. In fact, he was one of the first Chinese to be actively involved in the serious sport of body-building.

Over the years, we became quite interested in many sports-related subjects. We used to work out in Chinese gung-fu, jujitsu, and different types of martial arts related activities. In those times, I began to look at James as an older brother.

For his size, James was extremely strong and could perform some unique physical feats that just a few people could perform. One that I recall was his ability to perform the "hollow back" hand balancing. James could do dozens of them at a time when most people were lucky to do one or two.

He could perform squats and other types of weightlifting feats that were incredible for his size and stature.

James was very popular with most of the people of Oakland Chinatown and most knew him as the "Mayor of Chinatown" because of his outgoing and friendly personality.

This nickname was quite common in Oakland in those days. Because of his expertise in Chinese gung-fu and his like for body-building, among the people who associated with him in those areas, he also became known as the "Tiger." James was truly a fighter in every sense of the word.

In the years prior to his joining the service, we used to travel extensively to many of the sporting events that featured bodybuild-ing. On those occasions, James was a very interesting person to be with. He would joke and really enjoy life. It was a day-to-day experience for him.

James took me under his wing, imparted much knowledge pertaining to life in general, and helped me very much. He was a free-thinker.

Although I never personally met Bruce Lee, I know that those two guys were in tune to the same way of thinking. They were ahead of their time in the practice and development of Chinese gung-fu. Both of them were creative, proud of their physical abilities, and capable of introducing new and innovative ideas. They were forerunners in their respected field.

Ricky Ramirez

"He took off his jacket while he raised his bent arm and said, 'This is a sledgehammer, not an arm.'"

I first met James Yimm Lee when a close mutual friend by the name of Stanley Wong introduced him to me at my barbershop in Oakland. This was in 1962. The very first time that we met, I knew that James was a very likeable person and we hit it off really good. He was a carefree sort of guy who really enjoyed living life to its fullest. He was the type of guy who had a happy-go-lucky attitude and never had a bad word to say about anyone. I suppose that was the reason that we got along so well, because we thought and acted in many of the same ways and looked at life in this same manner.

Through our many, many conversations when he would visit the shop, I had the opportunity to share experiences and could relate to many of the same topics that were important to Jimmy. I was never one who was interested in martial arts, or gung-fu as Jimmy called it, but had some limited experience as a boxer when

I was younger. Our many conversations never dwelled on the
combative topics but more so
on family, sporting, and recre-
ational activities. For quite some
time, I never really knew that he
ever knew anything about the
martial arts. He was so congen-
ial and easygoing that no one
would have ever suspected that
he was so skilled in the art of
gung-fu. As our friendship grew,
James coined the nickname

"The Great Lover" for me. It all started out as a joke but after all of
these years the name has stuck. It's amazing how those kinds of
things happen.

I could always count on seeing Jimmy ever other week when
he would come in and get a trim. This would be the most time
that would ever elapse between the times that I would see him but
in most cases we were in constant contact whenever he was in the
downtown Oakland area, which was quite often.

I think we probably solved all of the world's problems in the
many years that we knew one another. We discussed virtually every
known topic other than the martial arts and I was really surprised
to find out that he was so skilled. What's more, I was flabbergasted
when he brought me several of his books and gave them to me. I was
astonished that Jimmy was so well known in the martial arts world.

I never will forget all of the times that we would socialize in the
San Francisco and Oakland Chinatown areas. Jimmy was quite well
known there and everywhere that we would go he was constantly

introducing me to new people. I must have met several thousand new acquaintances during that time.

It was in those initial get-togethers that I had the opportunity to meet Bruce Lee. Jimmy brought him by the barbershop for a haircut. Immediately, I could sense that Bruce was a sharp guy who was on the ball. He was a very sharp dresser with a smooth way of conversing.

He was an excellent physical specimen who carried himself very well. All of his casual physical mannerisms were very precise with very little waste of unnecessary motion. Jimmy introduced Bruce as his martial arts partner and roommate. Again, I was taken aback when I discovered that Bruce was a martial arts expert. Just like Jimmy, the looks were frightfully deceiving. At first, I had my doubts that Bruce could be so proficient, because he did not carry himself like a fighter. He did not have that stern personality that most people associate with fighters. Even his physique didn't reflect the characteristics of what most people assume are the marks of a fighter. His face was smooth with no scars or flattened nose or cauliflower ears or those sorts of things. The way that Jimmy and Bruce joked and kidded around you would have thought they were more into comedy than in the martial arts. Jimmy, Bruce, and myself would get into laughing so hard at the jokes that we shared that it's a wonder that our sides didn't split from it. It was hard to take anything too seriously when those guys were around.

I was totally shocked when I found out that Bruce was going into the television series and was becoming involved with the motion picture industry. He or Jimmy had never mentioned it. I think that they didn't want to boast or brag about plans in that way but let nature take its course. Even when they were in the shop it was not a major topic of conversation. I really knew that they were going for it and could tell that they were ready for anything that came their way.

After Bruce had departed for Hollywood to get involved with the films, Jimmy would always bring clippings and publicity into the shop so that I was kept up to date on Bruce's adventures.

As things were beginning to fall in place with Bruce's movie career, he would continually mention that as soon as he got in the position, he wanted Jimmy and myself to play parts in his films. This created a lot of excitement when James and myself would hear that.

I recall on one such visit that I jokingly mentioned to Bruce that he still did not look like the type who could convince the world that he was a gung-fu champion. Bruce just smiled and said that he was ready for it and he was in pretty good condition and could take care of the business if it became necessary. He then commenced to demonstrate his toughness by inviting me to punch his hand as hard as I could. I thought that he was kidding and said that I hit pretty hard from my boxing days and if I hit his hand it would probably break it. Bruce urged me to make the attempt to hit it as hard as I could and he promised not to move it when I began. I thought that Jimmy and Bruce may be pulling another practical joke on me but decided to go along with the scheme. As I wound up and delivered the punch, it hit with a resounding splat but it did not even faze Bruce. He didn't even flinch from the impact. This was convincing enough to me to prove that he had plenty of guts and could take what anyone could dish out.

On the times that Bruce was away, Jimmy and I still frequented many of the shops and restaurants in the Oakland area. Little by little, I was beginning to appreciate the real martial arts skill that James possessed even though he never displayed his fighting talents to me personally.

On one occasion, we were visiting a restaurant-bar in the downtown Oakland area. When we entered we immediately began to look for a seat. When we had sat down, a large truck driver entered and stood directly behind us and mentioned that he would not sit down next to a Chinese. This character stood about 6'4" and weighed in at about 240 pounds. I was a bit upset that this fellow was talking about Jimmy in that manner but Jimmy told me to relax and that everything would be all right. We then left the seats and moved down about ten or so seats and sat back down. Right after that the truck driver came on down and stood behind us and repeated his sarcastic speech.

In what must have been the blink of an eye, Jimmy cut loose on him with a backhand strike to the chest while still sitting in the chair. The driver hit the wall and then fell to the floor. He didn't even get up. Then Jimmy suggested that we evacuate the place before the law was called, so that we did with much haste. I was really excited and somewhat anxious with apprehension but Jimmy was so relaxed it was as if nothing had ever happened at all. This was the first time that I had seen him in action and I still couldn't believe my eyes. This small-framed guy really packed a tremendous amount of knockout power. When we got back to the barbershop, I asked Jimmy how he had done that and he mentioned that it all came from training and iron-palm techniques. He took off his jacket and displayed his muscular physique while he raised his bent arm and said, "This is a sledgehammer, not an arm." And that only comes from developing the body. There is no other way to achieve those types of techniques.

While Bruce was in Hollywood, James was always relating how Bruce wanted him to come down there. This was a sure indication that Jimmy and Bruce were strongly affected by the intentions of each other. On another instance when Bruce was up for a haircut he asked me if I was ready to go to Hong Kong to be in a film with Jimmy and himself. It didn't take long for me to reply, "You name the time and the date and I'll have my bags packed." It was nice to know that Bruce Lee thought so much of me as a friend. Although many of those later plans got canceled by a sequence of unfortunate events, I knew that his intentions were real and his sincerity was honest. This is the thing that true friendship is made of, and nothing can replace those sentiments.

Out of the many thousands of acquaintances that Jimmy had, I cannot help from thinking that I was probably the last person whom he had seen or talked to before his untimely death. I recall that we were having coffee at a nearby restaurant when Jimmy said that he didn't feel well and it felt like a spell was coming on and he thought that he would go home and take a bath and relax. This would relieve him and he could get some rest. The next thing that I knew, I had a call from his older brother Robert saying that James had just passed away. This was a complete and unsuspected shock and it felt like I had just lost a member of my own family.

I had not begun to get over the reality of Jimmy's demise when I got word that Bruce had died in Hong Kong while working on his newest motion picture.

It was so weird and almost mystical that two very close friends who had so much on the ball could die in such a very short period. Things were not supposed to happen that way. These close personal tragedies still affect me very much in more ways than most can imagine. These were two extremely close friends who shared a part of their life with a part of my life. There is no way to explain in words the deep hurt and the great loss that I have suffered.

To recount many of the treasured moments that we have spent

together brings back many of the small moments that seemed to be unimportant at the time. When you were there with them, you took it for granted, and when they are forever gone you really begin to realize how much you appreciated their company and friendship. That is something that everyone should learn at a very early age—to appreciate and enjoy each and every passing moment and never take anything for granted.

If they were here now, I would surely be much closer and would have taken the time to savor every one of those treasured moments. In closing, I can still see them smiling and joking and saying, "Everything is going to be OK. We'll see ya soon."

Aloy and Claire Brunk

"James Lee was a real blessing to our family. As the teacher of our daughter Sharon it was the knowledge that he taught her that saved her life."

James Lee was a real blessing to our family. As the teacher of our daughter Sharon it was the knowledge that he taught her that saved her life. Her ability to defend herself was indeed a treasure as well as a real blessing.

The first time that we had met James Lee, he had been teaching our daughter for several months. On this first occasion when he visited our home it was like we had known him for a long time.

We found him to be a very sincere and nice person who really cared for the happiness and welfare of others. With his warm personality we felt very close to him from the very first time that we met.

From the time of our first meeting, a strong bond of friendship and personal ties developed between James and his family and us and our family. The influence that he had on our daughter was one that gave her a true and real sense of confidence.

On the times that James would visit our home or when we would socialize, James would speak at great length about his philosophical views pertaining to the ancient ways taught by the gurus of Eastern civilizations. We shared many of the same beliefs on these topics. The innermost part of the soul and the role it plays in the physical realm was of strong interest to James and we could sense that he had a deep awareness of wisdom pertaining to a little-known subject.

At many of the social occasions, it was virtually impossible to treat James to dinners without his generosity overshadowing the entire event. When he could not get his way by covering the evening expenses he would purchase gifts for everyone to make up for his gracious and generous nature. He cared so much for people and always wanted to see everyone happy. He was such a giving man who wanted nothing in return.

The children played a very important part in James' life and he loved them so much. He would constantly talk about them and how proud he was of their scholastic accomplishments. His family and close friends meant a great deal to James and he was always willing to share everything with them while asking nothing in return. Their happiness was the only thing that really mattered.

James had a real zest for life and enjoyed being in the company of close friends and martial artists. He was a self-made man who knew what he was and who he was and found the biggest joy in being able to share with others. It was great that you could talk in a personal manner with him and sense that he really cared for you. He was a rare and wonderful individual.

The first time that we met Bruce Lee was through an introduction by James, and he was really proud that he could bring people together. Although we did not know Bruce very well, most of the children were quite excited about seeing or meeting him since he was a celebrity in television and motion pictures.

We could sense that James and Bruce were very close in the martial arts. Bruce gave the impression of being an intellectual individual who enjoyed the excitement of the spotlights whereas James was composed and content to just be relaxed and more down-to-earth with practical things.

James had a profound influence on Bruce in the same way that Bruce had an influence on James. There was a very strong and lasting friendship that bonded these two men. We felt that Bruce really needed the consciousness that James possessed, in much the same way that James needed the encouragement from Bruce. Together they were complete within the martial arts.

James never discussed being sick and it came as a total surprise when he called from the Doctor's Hospital. When James called from the hospital we immediately went to assist in any way that we could. He had a strong and willful determination that carried him through to the end. He tried not to let anything interrupt his plans for the future and was looking forward to going to Hong Kong to play a role in one of Bruce's movies, but fate prevailed and it never occurred. In retrospect, it was as if we had lost a close personal friend or immediate member of the family. He was very, very close.

The thought that James must have fulfilled his time on earth and has moved on to bigger things constantly enters our minds and he must have received a lot of love and admiration for the good that he did for others. When Bruce died it was like they were both together and that was the way that it was meant to be.

Dr. James Durkins

"The first time that I asked Bruce what gung-fu was all about, before you knew it he was giving me a firsthand demonstration. He could have kicked me three times before I could blink an eye."

I first met Bruce Lee on March 22, 1966, when he entered my optometrist office in San Leandro, California, to be fitted for his first set of contact lenses.

Upon examination, I discovered that Bruce had 20/400 vision in both eyes that had stemmed from myopia and astigmatism. Essentially, Bruce was very nearsighted and could see clearly only at a distance of two feet or less without the correction of glasses. Bruce was acutely aware of the need for contact lenses since he was then playing the part of "Kato" in *The Green Hornet* television series.

All of the action sequences that were required of his talents took much physical movement and since the hard contact lenses were just coming available to the general public, Bruce was totally in tune with the scientific breakthroughs that were happening in optometry. I recall the first time that I asked Bruce what this "gung-fu" was all about, and before you knew it he was giving me a first-hand demonstration. He could have kicked me three times before I could blink an eye.

It was upon Bruce's second visit to the office that about twenty or so young children flooded the office to get Bruce's autograph and to meet him for the first time. Bruce took the time to talk with them and I could tell that he really loved children.

He was very, very nice to those children and it impressed me tremendously.

Bruce introduced me to James Yimm Lee on one of the visits but I was not acquainted to any great extent; however, Bruce mentioned that he was excellent in the art of Chinese gung-fu.

Bruce Lee appeared to me to be a very intelligent young man who was extremely dedicated to what he did best, gung-fu.

When he was in Hollywood and even when he went to Hong Kong to make movies, he would constantly order new sets of contacts because he would lose them on the set when he was rehearsing fight scenes. I think that contact lenses were a godsend to him when it came to demonstrating and performing martial arts on the silver screen.

Dr. Lloyd A. Freitas

"I am so grateful that James Y. Lee introduced me to Bruce Lee. They taught the art

of gung-fu at the highest possible level and I am very thankful for that. I often think about their teachings. We had an outstanding class and the members were very dedicated, respectful, and thankful."

I have been a small-animal veterinarian in Oakland for several years. In addition, I have had many interesting and famous clients. It was on October 5, 1966, when James Y. Lee came into my office with his sick cat whose name was Kato. I treated his cat and we discussed the name Kato. I mentioned that Kato was the name of the Green Hornet's chauffeur on television. James Lee said, "Yes, and he is Bruce Lee and he is my friend." As we continued to talk, James Lee said he had been teaching gung-fu. He also said Bruce would be coming up from Los Angeles in two weeks and he would bring him into my office. At this point, I held my breath and said, "OK." During the following week, I decided to enroll in James Lee's gung-fu class. Incidentally, the cat got better.

Two weeks later when I was working in my office, in walks James with Bruce Lee. I was impressed. And from that moment on Bruce and I became good friends. When Bruce was in town, James would step aside and let Bruce—the Master—teach the class. You would know that Bruce could sense your next move and he would immediately have the counter to any move you would make. He was awesome. He often would say that his art was nonclassical—there was no system to what he taught! He would take each student aside and evaluate what the student could do. Then he would have the individual work on what would come naturally to that person. This was an excellent learning procedure for really become proficient in what Bruce wanted you to learn—expression of the self.

James Y. Lee was my Sifu and I continued to take lessons from him. He called me his virgin because I had no bad habits from any martial art system! I was able to progress rapidly in gung-fu as my athletic ability was still there from my school days when I had lettered in wrestling, football, and track.

I enjoyed hearing about Bruce's celebrity students in Los Angeles. To name a few: Steve McQueen, James Coburn, Kareem Abdul-Jabbar, Dean Martin Jr., Desi Arnaz Jr., Chuck Norris, and Joe Lewis. Bruce had the ability to see why one lost in a tournament. This happened several times when Chuck Norris would meet Joe Lewis. Bruce would work with the loser and in the next tournament, the loser would be the winner!

Bruce would tell us to practice the fundamentals repeatedly, and gradually you will be able to progress. In addition, he would tell us not to use what we learn to hurt anyone intentionally but only use it to defend yourself. And do not show off with your new knowledge. He told the students that learning to protect yourself would give you the confidence that hopefully you will never have to use it. Bruce was an excellent judge of people and knew which students he would spend more time with.

Bobo was Bruce's Great Dane and they would keep fit by running daily. She was a very friendly and loving dog and they had a good time together. When Bruce would come up to Oakland, he would leave Bobo at my hospital and we would enjoy her company.

I greatly enjoyed the teachings of Bruce Lee. He was a great teacher and philosopher. Bruce constantly reminded us about yin-yang—the flow of energy with no emptiness. He had several favorite expressions. For instance, "Have your movements flow smoothly like water" and "Bamboo is stronger than steel as it bends with the wind and does not break." He would say, "Be flexible. Stay focused. Use your opponent's energy to defeat him."

When I pulled a hamstring kicking, I was in pain and discomfort for some time. Bruce heard about my injury when he was in Los Angeles and was very kind to write me a letter to express his concern. He cared very much about his students and was sensitive to their misfortunes.

It was such a tragedy that Bruce died at such an early age of 32. He mentioned that he wanted to tell the world the truth about martial arts and what better way than the movies to reach millions of people. He would say that the producers would have him slow down his movements because they were too fast! Also, he was disappointed that Hollywood wanted to keep most of the revenue and not give him what he thought he should get. Therefore, Bruce went back to Hong Kong and was successful in working out a favorable deal with Golden Harvest Movie Studio.

I am so grateful that James Y. Lee introduced me to Bruce Lee. They taught the art of gung-fu at the highest possible level and I am very thankful for that. I often think about their teachings. We had an outstanding class and the members were very dedicated, respectful, and thankful.

I would say that Bruce Lee has been my most famous client. It was so special that I had the pleasure of getting to know him and he considered me his friend. I hope others appreciate all that he gave to his art of gung-fu for the world to see. He was way ahead of his time and very few, if any, will ever reach the height that he did.

Ming Lum

"James and Bruce both spoke Chinese and English very well and this perhaps contributed toward their ability to reach many different people who were interested in gung-fu."

The first time that I met James Lee was about 1957 when he was training in the sil lum gung-fu style. At the time, he was training under the guidance of Professor T.Y. Wong at his Chinese gung-fu kwoon on Waverly Place in San Francisco, California.

James was a very dedicated and serious martial artist who spent a lot of time improving and developing himself in the Chinese traditional martial arts.

Whenever I paid a visit to the kwoon, James was always there working out. This was normal for him, and he was there at least three or four times a week. At the time, there were only three of four martial arts schools around and James was one of the rare few who were dedicated to seeking out and learning this knowledge.

He was a very nice guy and we got along very well. During our many get-togethers we used to discuss the martial arts on many planes. James was always willing to learn any skills that could better himself. He was one of the best that I have ever seen in breaking techniques and it was not unusual for him to break bricks and boards with either hand. In the breaking demonstrations that he would perform, he would use the top of the palm, front of the palm, or chopping techniques—it really didn't matter to James.

He was also unique in the fact that he could select one brick out of a stack and only break the one that he selected. Very few people can do that type of breaking.

When I first met Bruce Lee, it was about 1962. He was a very strong young man and I could tell that he could handle himself very well. He could hold his own against anyone. Bruce used to perform at many of the local martial arts events and demonstrate his best skills. On one such occasion I recall telling him that he'd better do his best because there were a lot of martial artists there who wanted to see him perform. Bruce was quick to reply, "I'll do my best for you, Mr. Lum." In those times, there was a lot of professional jealousy within martial arts and there were quite a few people who both liked and disliked Bruce, but eventually it all balanced out.

There was a time when James and Bruce initially got together, began training, and opened a school that I did not see them as often. I could see that they both respected each other very much and spent a lot of time developing and modernizing the martial arts, as they knew them. They were great in their own unique way of training and blending the Eastern and Western martial art styles. I believe that they are the ones responsible for Westernizing the ways of teaching in the martial arts.

James and Bruce both spoke Chinese and English very well and this perhaps contributed toward their ability to reach many different people who were interested in gung-fu. At that time, karate seemed to be the big thing and not too much was known about the little-known art of Chinese gung-fu.

Bruce was very aggressive in this way and had a knack for reaching and communicating with people verbally and through his physical skills. Bruce and James were flexible with cultural differences. If they wanted to follow traditional Chinese traditions they could do that and if they wanted to follow traditional Western traditions, they could do that also. Some people liked them for that whereas others disliked their approach to teaching and presenting these relatively unknown styles of traditional arts. Other people's opinions did not seem to matter to Bruce and James and they continued to do things in the way that suited their needs.

It was Bruce who pushed Chinese into the Western world and I never thought that he and Chinese gung-fu would become as big as they have. I picture Bruce and James as two of the greatest men in martial arts. They combined the modern styles with the older and more traditional styles. Bruce became known worldwide whereas James was known predominately on the West Coast but probably with time, James would have been well known as well.

When Al Novak told me of James' death, I was totally shocked. Not long afterward, when I heard of Bruce Lee's death in Hong Kong, I was again very shocked but I suppose the whole world was shocked in the same way. We were very upset that we had lost two great men.

They were both great men who learned a lot from each other and will probably always be remembered as the two men who combined the older martial arts ways with the newer Western ways. I'm sure they will always be remembered for it.

Dr. Norman Marks

"Bruce Lee was a real champion! When he was in someone's presence, the atmosphere was

'electric' and it did not take long to realize that Bruce was a very positive person."

I first met James when he began working out in bodybuilding at my gym on Webster and 14th Street in Oakland. It was about 1955 and James was 35 years old at the time. During the next three to four years he would train intermittently but in that time we became very good friends. James was very outgoing and respected.

Whenever he would come into the gym to work out, he spent most of his training hours dedicated to hard work, and in most instances he preferred to train by himself. He trained very hard and never messed around with superficial conversation.

At times, after workouts, we would have friendly chats about the deeper meanings in and personal satisfactions received from bodybuilding. As I recall, James was a real innovator with the concepts of physiology. Everything that he did, he did it to the best of his ability. In all of the time that I knew him, never once did he display or mention his martial arts ability. I could sense that he was dedicated to his art without him ever performing martial arts. In the nearly twenty years that I knew James he was constantly enthused with bodybuilding and physical conditioning. He was a personable man who communicated very well on a one-on-one basis.

During the time that I knew James, I had the chance to meet Bruce on several occasions in Oakland. I was very much impressed that Bruce Lee was a real champion. When he was in someone's presence, the atmosphere around him was "electric" and it did not take long to realize that Bruce was a very positive person. For a person with his rare ability, I was truly impressed by his humble, soft-spoken attitude. He was very much a gentleman.

Sid Campbell

"*I must say that both Bruce and James Lee were real gentlemen and true martial artists. We all knew Wally Jay and thought he was a really great martial artist with a lot of respect for all styles of the fighting arts from all countries. There was no ego that got in the way of mutually sharing martial arts knowledge and techniques. Just like most everyone at that time, we all wanted to discover all we could about the differences and similarities between styles and different countries' approaches to self-defense in general.*"

Wally Jay was the very first person to mention James Yimm Lee and Bruce Lee to me back in the early part of 1966. This was when I had returned from Okinawa, Japan, and opened the very first Shorin-ryu (Kobayashi-ryu) Okinawan Karate School in the United States. In fact, Wally Jay was the first martial artist to visit my new school and welcome me to the Bay Area back in those early days.

He had mentioned that not too far away from me was a Chinese gung-fu man named Jimmy Lee. He had studied sil lum (Shaolin in Mandarin) and he was pretty good. Wally had men-

tioned that Jimmy had a training partner by the name of
Bruce Lee. Being new to the
Oakland area and just returning from Okinawa after serving my tour of duty in the
United States Navy and learning karate there, I was anxious
to meet other martial artists
who had knowledge of different styles.

My Shorin-ryu School had
been open for only several
months when two Chinese men dropped by in the early evening.
One was about my age (I was 22 then) and James Lee seemed about
40. They introduced themselves as Bruce Lee and James Lee. What
I thought was interesting is that the younger one, Bruce Lee, was
very inquisitive and forthright in asking a lot of questions about
Okinawan shorin-ryu karate. After reading the *kanji* (traditional
Japanese writing characters expressed with ancient Chinese
ideograms) on my 4th dan (degree) black belt certificate, which
hung proudly in my office, both Bruce and James noted similarities in the Chinese writing characters of sil lum and shorin-ryu
interpretations.

Soon thereafter, Bruce Lee wanted to see some of the Okinawan
shorin-ryu kata (forms). I demonstrated several of the *naihanchi*
kata and James looked on. Bruce then commenced to demonstrate
some of his forms of what I came to learn were wing chun. He
performed a set called *sil lim tao*. One thing that Bruce and James
noted was the similarity in concept, technique, and hand manip-

ulation of both styles; I was equally surprised to discover the similarities as well, since I had never seen any wing chun style.

These comparisons gave us a lot in common and Bruce was very interested in the quick, explosive hand techniques found in shorin-ryu. He had never heard of shorin-ryu until that day, but was very interested in everything that I had to say about the art of karate from Okinawa. I, too, was as interested and curious about this Chinese art of wing chun.

I must say that both Bruce and James Lee were real gentlemen and true martial artists. We all knew Wally Jay and thought he was a really great martial artist with a lot of respect for all styles of the fighting arts from all countries. There was no ego that got in the way of mutually sharing martial arts knowledge and techniques. Just like most everyone at that time, we all wanted to discover all we could about the differences and similarities between styles and different countries' approaches to self-defense in general.

I discovered that Bruce Lee was visiting his friend James Yimm Lee and that he had recently moved to Los Angeles. He said that he was a partner with James Lee in a school in Oakland and he traveled up to Oakland from time to time to teach and help with the instructional duties.

After this initial visit, I did not see Bruce Lee again in Oakland, but Jimmy Lee dropped by every now and then to say hello and watch some of my beginners classes. We would talk and share martial arts ideas, particularly concepts of in-close fighting. James would always tell me how he was building new equipment for gung-fu training, equipment that he believed did not exist anywhere else and that would help increase punching and striking skills.

Soon thereafter some of James Lee's students from the Monticello Avenue garage would drop by and introduce themselves and observe classes. I think James had suggested that they drop by my school to compare the differences and similarities of what they were learning. Many of these students of his have since become lifelong friends of mine. Richard Carney used to drop by all of the time and we would go out for lunch and chat for hours.

I had always known that Bruce, because of his keen interest and curiosity in the martial arts, would achieve success at teaching. He had a way of using philosophy to convey martial arts wisdom and to justify the purpose of fighting techniques. James, on the other hand, tended to be more direct and less eloquent with words. He would use simple statements of fact and then commence to demonstrate the function and purpose of fighting applications. It was James Lee who gave me the idea to set up hand-conditioning pots in my old Maple Avenue school in Oakland. One container had rice, one had beans, and the other had "BB" shot. For many years I had those pots in my dojo.

I must say that James Yimm Lee had the most conditioned hands of anyone I've ever known. His arms and hands were strong and toughened to the point where he could punch a cement wall and never even wince. I had trained on the *makiwara* punching board at the school in Okinawa for more than four years and had some pretty big calluses on my knuckles at the time. But James did not have any calluses and he could punch boards or bricks with no fear of damaging his hands. He had the best-conditioned hands of anyone I've ever seen, then or now.

I once mentioned that to Al Novak and he said, "Boy! Jimmy Lee was something else. He could break bricks and boards like nobody's business. He's the best that's ever been when it comes to iron-hand training."

I can see now, in retrospect, why Bruce Lee was such a close friend and confidant of James Lee, a man who had so much to offer in the way of practical experience, training knowledge, conditioning techniques, weight resistance science, and so forth.

Bruce could not help but learn from James Lee. James was truly Bruce Lee's mentor in more ways than anyone knew at that time. In fact, this relationship enabled the two to mature more rapidly and remarkably than if they had never met. Like the yin-yang dynamic, these two men complemented and balanced each other in such a unique way that each went on to achieve far more than they would have alone.

Eric Lee

"Oakland was my martial arts roots. Each teacher on the path I have traveled has given something valuable to me, and James Lee touched my life greatly. He was one of the vital influences in my martial arts development and I remember him with the utmost of honor and respect."

I am so happy that Sid Campbell and Greglon Yimm Lee are doing *Remembering the Master*. It was truly one of the most pivotal times in martial arts history.

We are all martial artists and love the art. Back in the early 1960s when I came to this country, being Chinese and having the first

inspiration from my dad who was a martial artist himself, I was quite the fanatic on the culture. There in Oakland, I met many fine martial arts instructors and eventually had my own martial arts club in Laney College. That was about the time when I first heard about Bruce Lee.

During the late 1960s I had the privilege of training with Sifu James Lee, who was one of Bruce's own students. He taught students jun fan gung-fu in his garage on Monticello Avenue. It was a wonderful experience. He always said what he felt. He was tough and sassy, never pulling any verbal punches! His physical punches were also so powerful with hands so tough from training iron-palm technique and working out on his homemade equipment. He was the innovator of such advanced ideas in training equipment that some of his creations are still being utilized today. Even though the time with him was too short, and sadly he is gone from us now, the memories are still alive in my heart.

Oakland was my martial arts roots. Each teacher on the path I have traveled has given something valuable to me, and James Lee touched my life greatly. He was one of the vital influences in my martial arts development and I remember him with the utmost of honor and respect.

Howard Williams

"Although my time with Bruce Lee was priceless, it was James Lee who instilled in me all the principles and teachings of the original art."

It was James Lee whom I spent most of my years with. Not enough is said about James Lee as a person and martial artist. Being thrown into the advanced class as a young kid fresh off the streets ... he could have easily allowed me to become overwhelmed and discouraged. But instead, he helped and guided me through the more difficult times, while reassuring me that through repetition and hard work, jeet kune do would soon become a natural part of my life. James Lee was a traditional martial arts master, using modern tools to teach with. With that same gung-fu tradition, he used those modern tools to help mold and cultivate me in the original framework of jeet kune do, the way he and Bruce had intended it should be.

Although my time with Bruce Lee was priceless, it was James Lee who instilled in me all the principles and teachings of the original art.

Al Dacascos

"Staying at Linda Lee's house, I was given access to all of Bruce's training equipment, books, clothing, and even driving his right-side Mercedes-Benz convertible sports car. I had to get into the spirit of Bruce. Linda offered me all of Bruce's clothing and footwear if I wanted it. I told her that it would be nice but Bruce was 5'7" and 140 pounds, but I was 5'9" and now weighing in at 155 pounds. He wore a 7 ½ and I wore a size 9 ½ shoe so I declined the offer. Now that I think about it, it would have been worth a lot to somebody who may have wanted it for a museum presentation."

Did I know the direction my life would take and how a Chinese person by the name of Bruce Lee would have a profound and lasting influence in the way I did my martial arts? Hell, no! I went about my business of doing things my way, the *kajukenbo-tum-pai* way with the Sid Asuncion kempo mentality.

Arriving in San Francisco, California, in 1966 from Honolulu during the month of February did little to convince me that I should stay and make my home on the Mainland. It was freaking cold and

my blood was too thin to accept the bone-piercing, chilling breeze that crept over the mountains to Daly City, California, which was home for a few weeks. My older brother George lived there and was delighted that another one of the family dared to venture out of the island paradise I call Hawai'i. I have never seen frost on cars in the morning, ice on the lawns that crinkled when you walked on it, steam coming out of your breath, and the Bay Area fog blinding you as you drove in traffic. I never was fully prepared to wear thermal underwear; and for me during those first few weeks, I wore thermal on top of thermal and made my skinny frame of 140 pounds look like I was 160 pounds. My wife then, Mariko, and my son Mark, who had just turned 2 years old a few days earlier, came a couple of weeks after me. They got off the jet from sunny Hawai'i into the San Francisco evening breeze and their eyes shot wide open as the air attacked their clothing.

I do not know what Bruce Lee was doing during that time but I was ready to make my move to the other side of the bay, toward Hayward, California. I was informed it was warmer and besides, I had a high school classmate living in the Hayward-Oakland area who wanted to learn martial arts. My brother wanted me to stay in the San Francisco area. He had already scheduled an interview for me with the plumbing company he was working at as an estimator. Melvin Abero, who convinced me to interview for a job at Western Electric in San Leandro, already had put in good words for me at that place where he worked. He and I corresponded while I was still in Honolulu, Hawai'i, learning kajukenbo from Sifu Sid Asuncion by way of mail. Since my marriage was on the rocks... literally, I made the decision that if my marriage was going to survive, I had to move to the Mainland. I worked two jobs just to accumulate the funds to move my family, giving up a position as assistant manager to the first Sizzler Steak House in Hawai'i, and as a stock clerk for Tandy's Toys for Men.

The small group of kempo students that I was teaching at the beach park was for fun and that was not going to keep me back in Hawai'i. One of them, Douglas Espinda, would follow me a few months later to Hayward, California. My first group of six students met at a friend's house in Union City, California. We outgrew the garage in a couple months and found a dance studio called Cherryland Hall in Hayward. It was here in Cherryland Hall that I was confronted with a small group of representatives from the San Francisco Chinese kung-fu communities. In no uncertain terms, they told me that I should not be teaching Occidentals. It seemed to me like a challenge but they soon backed down when they noticed my demeanor as a representative of Adriano D. Emperado's Kajukenbo Institute of Self Defense of Hawai'i during one of my training sessions. It was also at Cherryland Hall that, through one of my students, I met Ron Lew, who would introduce me to Sifu Paul Ng in San Jose. This led me to continue my training in the Chinese martial arts. Paul Ng was having training sessions with another famous kung-fu instructor in San Francisco. At the same time, Ming Lum, a very well-known personality in what we called the underground Chinese community in San Francisco and a transplanted Hawai'ian-Chinese, an advisor to Emperado at that time, introduced me to Professor Wong Jack Man, Paul Ng's Northern style kung-fu instructor. A couple of weeks later I was to find out that the incident that happened to me in my school had happened to Bruce Lee a few years earlier, except that Wong Jack Man was the individual selected to confront Bruce Lee, in that famous fight at Bruce Lee and James Yimm Lee's Oakland kwoon.

Cherryland Hall is where we grew from a small group to slightly over forty students within a year of being there. Now it was time to look for another location and we found one on East 14th Street in San Leandro, California.

Bruce Lee and James Lee's names kept popping up in casual conversations especially after tournaments in the Bay Area. I was getting involved with tournament competition and my students were doing quite well. Most were being disqualified for excessive contact and it was not their fault. It was the way that I was training them. Being in San Leandro and on one of the main boulevards drew curiosity among those vaguely aware of martial arts. I had a huge black pagoda as the entrance to my school with a sign that said "School of Chinese Kempo Gung-fu." In those days, not too many people knew what Chinese kempo was, let alone gung-fu. Some people thought that it was a school to teach Chinese cooking and most did not know anything at all. I would see people peeping in the darkened windows to see what was happening inside. As a matter of fact, I gained lots of new students that way. Then, one day, as I was cleaning the darkened training hall on a weekend afternoon, I noticed two Chinese men looking in the window. They stared through the front window a bit while talking between themselves. Not thinking anyone was inside, the men finally decided to leave. It dawned on me as they walked toward their car that I recognized both of them from a book that a student had given me a couple of weeks earlier. It was a beige-covered book titled *Chinese Gung-Fu: The Philosophical Art of Self-Defense* and had been written by a fellow named Bruce Lee, and he and the other fellow were photographically featured performing gung-fu in the book. My curiosity was really piqued as to why such honored visitors would have come during the time that I had posted the closed sign on my front door so I could clean up the kwoon.

A few weeks after, my students and I did a demonstration in the Oakland Auditorium during the Summer Home and Garden Show exhibit. There again were these two Chinese men sitting in the first row. One of them, a skinny, handsome young man, sat with his legs and arms crossed, and the other older person smoked his cigarette. They watched our demo from beginning to end. When the next martial arts group came up to do their act, they politely left. I was told by a guest at the show that one of the fellows was a gung-fu teacher teaching wing chun in the Oakland hills. I never heard of that art and was more curious to know who this person was.

A couple of weeks passed, then we did another demonstration at a Teenage Fair. That was when the sparks began to fly. It was there after the fair had concluded that my student, then a green or a brown sash, by the name of Ted Sotelo got into a verbal confrontation with two of James Lee's students over who and what style was better. Like all students, they are proud of their own instructor and style. Ted and his brother Bobby were two of my very best students and it was obvious that I favored both of them. Bobby was about 12 or 13 years old and Teddy 17 or 18 years old then and these two boys must have made impressions on Bruce and James Lee during one of our demonstrations. Their names keep popping up as faces to watch. In this confrontation between

Teddy and James Lee's students, the name of Al was brought up as the only person who had knocked Bruce Lee off his "horse." I was supposed to have a friendly meeting with Bruce Lee after the fair but Bruce canceled it. I guess he was angry with me from what he heard about me knocking him off his horse. I was upset that Bruce did not want to talk to me but had no idea the reason he called off our meeting. When I found out that it was Teddy who had this confrontation with James Lee's students, I told Teddy to go straighten that out with James and Bruce. Ted went to James Lee's house and told James that there was a misunderstanding between Bruce and me. Bruce was in another room while James Lee and Teddy talked. Teddy was young and eager to learn more as James invited Teddy to show his stuff. Bruce intervened and wanted to see how Teddy would block a certain punch that he threw. When Teddy parried to the side and countered, Bruce was surprised that Teddy moved so well. Naturally, Teddy responded that it was Sifu Al Dacascos who trained all his students that way. Teddy told me that he was not sure at first that it was Bruce because of the thick glasses he was wearing at that time.

About the incident of Bruce Lee and Sifu Al? It came to be found out that Teddy was referring to Sifu Al Novak, who had knocked Bruce Lee off his horse with a punch to Bruce's chest a few months earlier. Those two students never connected the name of Al Novak as the culprit. Teddy had heard this from a friend of James Lee by the name of Newt Kamikani, who witnessed the event between Sifu Al Novak and Bruce Lee. When Teddy mentioned this event to those two students, they assumed that it was Sifu Al Dacascos and Bruce Lee. With the loud music of the band blaring and the boisterous crowd in the background, those two students did not hear right. I went to James Lee's house myself a few weeks later to settle this rumor because it had not stopped. I had heard that Bruce was in Oakland during a short break in shooting *The Green Hornet* TV series for ABC (1966–1967).

I introduced myself to James Lee, who already was very familiar with me, and told him that I came to clear this rumor up. James was very hospitable but told me that Bruce was not there and had been delayed but that he would convey the message to Bruce when he came up to Oakland. I was determined to make sure there were no hostility between Bruce and me. I guess the time was not in my cards to meet Bruce just yet. Instead, I met Bobby Baker, then a student of Bruce and James and at one time a student of my instructor Sid Asuncion and me back in Hawai'i. Bobby Baker would be the person holding the pad at the International Karate Championships in Long Beach where Bruce did his famous one-inch punch that sent Bobby flying back a few yards. I was surprised and happy for Bobby Baker having continued his training in the martial arts after serving his time in the Navy stationed at Pearl Harbor, Hawai'i. He was very concerned with finding any art similar to what we were teaching back then on Oahu.

I met Bruce Lee face-to-face for the first time at Ed Parker's 1967 International Karate Championships in Long Beach, California. After months of seeing each other from a distance and hearing of him and about the rumors that were flying back and forth, this would be the first of a few more meetings to come. The year before at the 1966 International Karate Championships, I was competing in the tournament in forms. Bruce was sitting in the front row to the stage where the final contestants from the Chinese, Korean, and Japanese first-place winners were to compete for the grand championship. John Pereira represented the Japanese forms, Chuck Norris represented the Korean style, and I represented the Chinese style. I had torn my left hamstring muscle while warming up for the evening finals, and John Pereira took the grand championship in kata that night. Bruce was cheering for me and still we had not talked yet. I cannot remember who won the fighting *(kumite)* grand champion title but I think it might have been Chuck Norris. However, this year of 1967 was different.

Bruce Lee's name had become bigger than ever at the time. His *Green Hornet* television series was doing well and he was appearing in martial arts magazines more often, while giving gung-fu and karate exposure never enjoyed previously. Even his tournament appearances were more frequent, and people came to these events just to see and hopefully meet him. Both of us were promoting gung-fu, only in different ways. He was doing it in the entertainment arena and I was doing it on the national tournament circuit by performing demonstrations. Many of my performances were in forms and multiple-opponent fighting along the West Coast of the United States. I also competed in forms under the Chinese gung-fu banner and fighting as a kajukenbo *ch'uan-fa* stylist. My *wun hop kuen do* expression had not been named yet and it was still a couple of years away. Because of my Chinese forms, my own personal way of fighting, the public looked at me as a gung-fu fighter instead of kajukenbo. This drew a lot of interest in the Chinese martial arts communities, because there was no one Chinese fighter winning in those early tournament years. In fact, most of them were being creamed. Our School of Chinese Kempo Gung-fu drew a lot of unwanted attention during those days. Our black *jing-mo* uniform, fast lead-side back fist, left reverse punch, lead-side, side-, and round kick, drop kicks to the groin, and rapid hand combinations became our trademarks. I am sure that Bruce was curious to see how far Al Dacascos would go in competition as a Chinese gung-fu fighter going up against the other stylist. Years later after Bruce Lee had passed on, I would find out after being invited to stay at Linda Lee's house while auditioning for *The Life and Legend of Bruce Lee* movie. Two decades later, it would be called *Dragon: The Bruce Lee Story* starring Jason Scott Lee. As the evening wore off at the 1967 Internationals, Bruce Lee—elegantly suited in his blue blazer, turtleneck, and white pants— was in the hallway to the exit. I had just changed out of my jing-mo gung-fu uniform and came out of the dressing room when we bumped into each other. I said, "Hi, Bruce." He replied and from that point on our acquaintance had finally begun. I told him that for the last year, there had been many rumors going around in the Oakland Bay Area concerning us. He cut me off and told me, "Instructors don't make problems for each other; students do. So don't worry about it." Those were comforting words to my ears. It would have been nice to have had that behind us from the beginning instead of thinking about it the whole year. Instead of departing then, we somehow ended up in the lobby talking for the next hour or so on techniques and training methods. Bruce went on to do bigger and better things as his career took a turn for him to be in Hong Kong. As for me, I moved to Denver, Colorado, in 1969 and used it as a center point from which to travel to more states to compete.

The next time we would meet would be at a team competition where I fought with the Midwest team going up against a team that Fumio Demura had put together. Bruce Lee was sitting at ringside. I was pitted against a 5th or 6th degree black belt in Japanese style. He was fresh from Japan and eager to see what we American fighters could do. There were other teams there also. The Tracy's team was led by Joe Lewis, while Chuck Norris led his team. There was also a team from the East Coast, one from Texas, and a team from the Chicago Great Lakes area. When our team came up to fight, we were pitted to fight the Japanese team. I was the second to fight in a five-man team. It was a total point accumulation sort of tournament, and I scored five points on my Japanese opponent to his zero. On one attack, I lunged in with a back fist, reverse punch, and spinning back kick that sent my opponent into the lap of Bruce Lee. As the opponent got off Bruce Lee, Bruce smiled and gave me the thumbs-up. My fighting style had changed and I was using a right lead forward, right arm hanging, left hand on the side of my face to cover or parry. Again, we chatted after the fights, and Bruce asked me why I like coming out that way. I told him that traditionally, I used to come up with my two hands guarded high but that all changed when in a competition against a Korean *tae kwon do* fighter from Los Angeles, he slipped in a side-kick to my ribs that sent me flying into the judges' table. I never went out that way again and I developed the closed-in guard method for my personal safety. That guarded position became another trademark of my wun hop kuen do (WHKD) tournament fighters and it worked for them too. A year or two later, I would see that posture in Bruce's posters and films. Then I smiled and wondered to myself where he picked that up.

I was sitting down watching television one evening with my family in July 1973, and the news flashed across the television screen about Bruce's death. Like the rest of the martial arts world, we were saddened and shocked. A group of us from Denver and some of my gung-fu instructor friends from San Francisco flew to Hong Kong and witnessed the post-funeral chaos among the news media, claiming they knew the inside story of Bruce's death. Many magazines and newspapers made fortunes on anything surrounding the mystery of Bruce's passing, as well as many rip-off movies on Bruce Lee.

A year later, 1974, Mike Anderson formed a group of United

States martial artists, representing the top fighters and masters in the Asian fighting arts, to tour several cities in Europe. My wife Malia and I were among the names in the gung-fu world then. Malia and I had just finished an appearance on Merv Griffin's TV show with Joe Lewis and Howard Jackson. Joe Lewis had mentioned on national TV that Al Dacascos was the king of gung-fu after Bruce Lee passed away. Linda Lee was upset with that comment made, and I assured her that I knew nothing of what Joe Lewis was going to say. The relationship between Linda Lee and Malia grew as we spent the next three weeks in Europe together with Mike Anderson's tour. After our return to America, Linda Lee invited Malia and me for a short stay at her house. She wanted me to review some materials that Bruce had in his file cabinet because there was a great interest in having his life's work published through *Black Belt* magazine. I told her I would look at it and give her my opinion. After seeing it, I told her she had better get people like Dan Inosanto and Bruce's first students involved. When I asked her why she wanted me to review it, she replied in confidence that Bruce had high respect for me and that I was not just talking, but was out there proving it. That made my day. When she wrote her book on Bruce called *The Man Only I Knew,* she made Bruce's comment on me public.

I returned to Europe a few months later on contract teaching in Hamburg, Germany, promoting gung-fu. Linda tracked me down and told me to fly to Hollywood immediately and audition for a possible movie. She said Hollywood had already done a worldwide search in major cities looking for the person to portray Bruce Lee. I told her that I was not interested but she insisted I do it. "Why?" I asked. Her reply was that none of the others could play the part, but she knew I could mimic Bruce's movements and be convincing. A few days later, I was at her house again, reading the script and readying myself for the screen test. Those next few days in Hollywood, California, would be the craziest period in my life. Staying at Linda Lee's house, I was given access to all of Bruce's training equipment, books, clothing, and even driving his right-side Mercedes-Benz convertible sports car. I had to get into the spirit of Bruce. Linda offered me all of Bruce's clothing and footwear if I wanted it. I told her that it would be nice but Bruce was 5'7" and 140 pounds, but I was 5'9" and now weighing in at 155 pounds. He wore a 7½ and I wore a size 9½ shoe so I declined the offer. Now that I think about it, it would have been worth a lot to somebody who may have wanted it for a museum presentation. Instead, I accepted four separate pieces of workout and training equipment but, regrettably, those items later disappeared when fans found out it first belonged to Bruce Lee. Likewise, two photos of Bruce and me together taken after the 1967 Internationals suddenly grew feet and walked off. I have a suspicion of who got it but cannot find him.

After passing the screen test at United Artists' Burbank sound studio with Howard Jackson as my counterpart, Robert Clouse, the director of *Enter the Dragon,* told me that I was it and the next thing to do would be to get William Morris Talent Agency to sign me. That was the easy part. What happened in the next couple of days sealed my destiny. Since Mike Anderson, Don Quine, and Judy Quine were involved with the Professional Karate Association circuit and promoted me with their *Professional Karate Magazine,* PKA president Don Quine felt that he should be my agent and manager. Linda Lee urged me to stay the course with William Morris, and now the backstabbing to get me to sign began. I had just come back from taking photo shots for *Inside Kung-Fu* magazine with Curtis Wong concerning the announcement of me being the lead for the movie. The political bickering over who should be my manager, my agent, and the fight-scene choreographer did nothing but stall that project. Fight choreographer Pat Johnson was hired to work with me on the project. I guess I felt insulted that a *tang soo do* stylist was going to direct me, a gung-fu stylist, on how to duplicate Bruce Lee's moments. This did not sit well with the staff, but I did not know it as I made my voice heard. I wanted to make sure they knew that I was not the "new Bruce Lee." They had wanted me to take up a more Chinese-American name. I wanted to be left alone as Al Dacascos portraying the life and legend of Bruce Lee. After months of negotiating, they decided to go with Alex Kwok out of Alberta, Canada, for the project. As history shows, the project sat on the shelf for nearly two decades before it came to life again.

During that time, Linda Lee and her family kept in touch with us in Denver, and Linda and her children, Shannon and Brandon, visited us a couple of times to go skiing. Likewise, we visited them in California. Brandon and Mark became friends, and that extended into their adulthood. When the news reached us of Brandon's death while shooting *The Crow*, we were traumatized. One day in 1991, my son Mark telephoned me and said that he was called to look at the script and see if he was interested in auditioning for the part of Bruce Lee for the movie called *Dragon*, re-titled from *The Life and Legend of Bruce Lee*. Mark wanted to know why it was not done and why I had declined to take the movie role back in 1975. I told Mark there could only be one Bruce Lee and besides, I did not want to change my name. Mark told me that my answer was good enough and he would decline the offer. Mark said he had another option and that was a movie on capoeira called *Only the Strong*, for which he was also asked to audition. "Take it, Mark," I said. I knew this film would make Mark instead of being labeled another Bruce Lee. When the TV project for *The Crow: Stairway to Heaven* came out, Mark hesitated and we consulted each other before he finally gave way to doing it. He did not want to do a bad presentation, because it was Brandon Lee's TV project at first. After a long year of doing the series, and a fatality on the set, Mark called it quits and moved on to other projects. As for me, I moved back to Hawai'i to sun and surf more than kick and punch. As for Bruce Lee, the life and the legend? He is a legend that helped change the way martial arts is perceived and practiced today.

Hank Maguire

"At that time, I did not know just how good Bruce was at gung-fu. Bruce Lee was going to school in Seattle, Washington. About two months later, I met Bruce Lee for the first time. I thought he was a real nice, clean-cut kid, and very respectful of people he met."

I first got into the martial arts in 1951 while actively serving in the United States Marine Corps and was introduced to jujitsu and have done martial arts all of my life. I wanted to study gung-fu, but in 1954, it was not being taught to the lo-fan [foreigners]. I had many Asian friends who also tried to find me a Sifu who would take me as a student. I was working out at Walter Todd's International Judo and Karate School in Oakland, California. One of my friends told me that he was studying wing chun gung-fu with a Sifu named Mr. James Lee. I asked him if he would introduce me to Sifu James Lee.

I met Sifu James Lee in 1961 at his home on Monticello Avenue in the Lake Merritt District in Oakland. He had a very special selected group of students he trained there. He was teaching the old art of wing chun gung-fu. He let me visit him for six months before he ever talked about gung-fu. We became very good friends and I met his son Greglon Yimm Lee. To this day Greglon and I are still very close friends.

One day, Jimmy and I were sitting watching television in his basement. He grabbed my fist and said, "Hank, I like you and I'm going to teach you gung-fu."

Mr. James Lee's kwoon was in his garage on Monticello Avenue. There on his wall he had a large poster of his close friend Bruce Lee. He told me that Bruce was coming to visit him and that I would meet him. At that time, I did not know just how good Bruce was at gung-fu. Bruce Lee was going to school in Seattle, Washington. About two months later, I met Bruce Lee for the first time. I thought he was a real nice, clean-cut kid, and very respectful of people he met.

In 1963, Bruce Lee and his wife Linda moved to Oakland and lived with James Yimm Lee and his family. It was there that their son Brandon was born. They were a real nice family. Greglon called Bruce "Uncle." So I used to call him "Uncle" Bruce too. Although Bruce was not my Sifu, we still spent time talking about gung-fu and what it meant to him. He told me one day as we ate some wonton soup that Bruce had cooked, "Hank, gung-fu is an obsession with me." He was very devoted to the art. He did teach me a lot by just watching him and Jimmy working out. He then started teaching private lessons at night. There was a chain of hot dog stands called Doggie Diner in San Francisco. Bruce taught self-defense to the night managers.

Bruce Lee and Sifu James Lee opened their first gung-fu kwoon (school) on Broadway in Oakland, about four blocks north of Oakland Technical High School. The kwoon was doing very good. After a time Bruce got his big chance to go to Hollywood. He was going to be Charlie Chan's number one son. However, that series never materialized. Then he was cast to play the role of "Kato" on *The Green Hornet*. You know the rest. It was an honor to have known my Sifu James Lee. I was always faithful to my Sifu. I never looked beyond what he taught me.

Mr. Bruce Lee was the best I have ever known. I shall never forget these friends in my life. As Greglon says, to me very often, "Hank, we knew the best. We knew the dragon and the tiger."

Joseph "Joe" Davis

"The martial arts world owes a great debt to Sifu Bruce Lee and Sifu James Yimm Lee,

as they are the ones who opened the door to the Chinese martial arts to the rest of the world, and in doing so, opened their minds to cross-training."

I trained in the old Jun Fan Gung Fu Institute in Oakland, California, from late 1964 until early 1965. The art was called "jun fan gung-fu," not jeet kune do. I lived in Fairfield, California, about forty miles away, and just being married I stop training after about five to six months. The fee was only $15 per month not the thousands that they were paying later down in Hollywood.

I do not remember many of the other students as it was forty years ago but one of them was a man named Elias Rodriguez; I believe he was "Mr. America" in 1954. Jack LaLanne came in second that year.

Sifu Bruce and Sifu James were teaching people other than Chinese but at this time we were only being taught the self-defense techniques; Sifu James would take the Chinese students into the back room to be taught forms. A lot of the training was not just physical but was mental. As you were working out Sifu Bruce would walk around the room and sometimes when he was behind you he would call out your name. And if you just turned around and looked without being aware, he would strike you lightly across the face and say, "Too slow." Sometimes when he called out your name and if you turned around and acted in an aggressive manner, he would say, "Why are you attacking me? I did nothing to you."

After class he would talk about the training; what he was trying to teach was to make you aware of dangers in your environment, but not to act in an aggressive manner to any sudden movements by other people. In addition, as he was walking around the room the students would try to watch him so sometimes you would be distracted and be struck by your training partner. Sifu Bruce would say that this was part of your training so that you would not be distracted and lose focus on your attacker.

Many of the students would ask about fighting in the street and using high kicks to the opponent's head. Sifu Bruce would say to kick them in the head, first kick them in the groin or knees, then when they bend over, kick them in the head. In the street you should not kick above the waist.

Sifu Bruce said that each movement has a flowing continuity without any dislocation. Simplicity is the key word to his art and the techniques should be smooth, short, and extremely fast, using a straight-line punching attack. Unlike most of the hard-line arts, he used a soft stance with the power hand forward. That is the stance that I still use today even thought I am a hard-line kajukenbo stylist, and I still teach my students to fight with the power hand forward and not from the old hard stances.

Some of the things that I remember other than the training: Sometimes Sifu James would demonstrate his breaking ability.

There was a movie called *Bad Day at Black Rock* that had a fight scene between a one-armed aikidoist (Spencer Tracy) and an attacker with a knife (Ernest Borgnine). Sifu Bruce said that was his favorite fight scene, so one night we stopped the class a little early and went over to the house of one of the students to watch the movie on television.

Kajukenbo Sifu Tony Ramos had a Hawai'ian luau in 1965, where Sifu James Lee and his students were doing a demonstration. Sifu Bruce was asked to demonstrate his one-inch punch; because I trained with him he used me to demonstrate the power of the punch and he knocked me back and into a chair. (Somewhere my ex-wife has a picture of that demonstration.)

I did not train very long with Sifu Bruce, but early on I realized that even with all of his movies that showcased martial arts (more so than his physical abilities), he stressed the philosophy of teaching one not to be trapped in a rigid system that does not allow an individual the freedom to express his or her own ability. That way the practitioner could strive and learn more. I believe this is the most important contribution that Sifu Bruce brought to the martial arts world.

The martial arts world owes a great debt to Sifu Bruce Lee and Sifu James Yimm Lee, as they are the ones who opened the door to the Chinese martial arts to the rest of the world, and in doing so, opened their minds to cross-training.

Even after forty years, I still have a receipt signed by Sifu Bruce Lee, the booklet, and an original brochure from 1964.

Richard Siu

"I remember Bruce. What was my first impression of Sibok Bruce Lee? Not so much an impression but a learning experience. He was a man who broke barriers. Here was an Asian man who had married a non-Asian at a time when Asians only

*married Asians.
Now I knew
anything was
possible and I
could do it all."*

My first impression of Greg's dad was that James was a good man. He was a good father, husband, and neighbor. His home was a place I could hang out and play. It was not until I was lining our garden with half-broken bricks that I discovered James was a martial artist. James was a gung-fu iron-hand master. I would watch James break multiple bricks and be amazed at the power of his hand, but even more amazing was that James had no calluses and how soft his hands were. It would be a decade later that I would also call him Sifu.

James had a good heart; not too many people would open their home to a family but that is what he did. He opened his home and befriended Bruce Lee and his family.

I remember Bruce. What was my first impression of Sibok Bruce Lee? Not so much an impression but a learning experience. He was a man who broke barriers. Here was an Asian man who had married a non-Asian at a time when Asians only married Asians. Now I knew anything was possible and I could do it all.

As a martial artist, Bruce was always impressive. He had speed and control. During one demonstration, he used my brother, Curtis Siu, as the target, standing a full six feet apart; Bruce bridged the distance in one movement, did a full side-kick, and left a smudge on my brother's nose. Later, I asked my brother what he saw; he said it happened so quickly, it was just one quick blur of a motion.

Yes, I remember Sifu and Sibok, from a longtime neighbor.

Richard K. Siu

■ Comrades Allen Joe, Bruce Lee, and James Yimm Lee celebrate Christmas in the San Francisco Bay Area.

■ Bruce Lee (left) and James Yimm Lee at the Red Lantern Restaurant in Oakland Chinatown. They would celebrate birthdays, have parties, and dine there with their students during the Oakland years (1962–1965).

■ Bruce Lee celebrating Christmas at Allen Joe's home in the Bay Area. Joe's son stands proudly at "Uncle Bruce's" side.

■ Bruce Lee (left), Dan Inosanto (middle), and Allen Joe (right).

■ Allen Joe and Bruce Lee at Joe's grocery store in Oakland, California. When Bruce and Linda lived in Oakland, Bruce and Allen would spend a lot of time together training and sharing bodybuilding knowledge.

■ Allen Joe and Bruce Lee at the newly opened kwoon in Los Angeles, California.

■ Bruce Lee learning to break boards with kicking techniques under James Yimm Lee's watchful supervision. Bruce was fascinated that James Yimm Lee could break enormous stacks of cement blocks with no apparent damage to his hands.

■ James Yimm Lee's student Al Novak breaking a stack of cement blocks with the back of his bare hand.

■ Al Novak and co-author Greglon Lee reminisce about the early Oakland years before the world knew about Chinese gung-fu.

Chinese Gung Fu Center

" The Philosophical Art of Self Defense "

Private Class Instruction for MEN, WOMEN and CHILDREN

FOR HEALTH
BODY CONDITIONING
SELF PROTECTION

No Falls, No Throws, No Strain, No Pain

26663 MISSION BLVD.
Hayward, California

6-6139

INSTRUCTORS
J.Y. Lee
A.L. Novak

■ James Yimm Lee and Al Novak's business card for the Chinese Gung Fu Center in Hayward, California, when they ran a school together.

■ Al Novak in his early 20s training in bodybuilding. Many of the students and friends of James Yimm Lee trained in bodybuilding long before it was popular to do so.

■ Al Novak celebrating his birthday at the World Martial Arts Masters Association Hall of Fame in 2004 in Castro Valley, California. Martial arts masters Eric Lee, Dan Tosh, and Jimmie Willis look on as Al Novak cuts his cake.

■ Longtime students of Bruce Lee and
James Yimm Lee, Felix Macias, Sr. (left)
and Al Novak (right).

■ Felix Macias, Sr., trains with his student Robert Fong.

■ James Yimm Lee (left) with his student Felix Macias, Sr., in 1968. Front row: Felix's sons (left) Felix, Jr., and (right) Larry Macias.

■ Student Gary Dill (left) with his teacher James Yimm Lee.

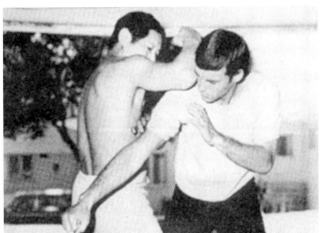

■ James Yimm Lee training with David Cox at James' 3039 Monticello Avenue home in Oakland, California.

■ James Yimm Lee (center, front row) and Bruce Lee (center, back row) with a cadre of their students at James' home in Oakland, California.

■ Wally Jay, a close friend and confidant to both Bruce Lee and James Yimm Lee. Bruce Lee discovered early on after traveling to Oakland, California, to share knowledge with James Yimm Lee that Wally Jay was the very best at judo and jujitsu, and Bruce would spend much time with him learning about those arts.

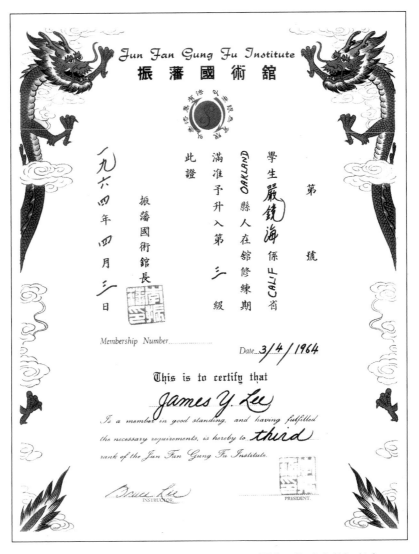

Jun Fan Gung Fu Institute

振藩國術館

學生 嚴鏡海 係 CALIF 省 OAKLAND 縣人在館修練期滿准予升入第三級此證

一九六四年四月三日

振藩國術館長

第　號

Membership Number

Date 3/4/1964

This is to certify that

James Y. Lee

Is a member in good standing, and having fulfilled the necessary requirements, is hereby to *third* rank of the Jun Fan Gung Fu Institute.

Bruce Lee
INSTRUCTOR.

PRESIDENT.

■ James Yimm Lee's third rank in Bruce Lee's Jun Fan Gung Fu Institute. It is one of the rare few official rank certifications that Bruce Lee actually signed and issued to his students.

EXCLUSIVE WOMENS CLASSES

JUN FAN GUNG FU INSTITUTE

TUES. & THUR. 7-8 pm

INSTRUCTION
IN THE CHINESE WING CHUN
ART OF SELF-DEFENSE

HEALTH PROMOTION, CULTIVATION OF MIND
SELF PROTECTION

■ The original Jun Fan Gung Fu sign used at Bruce Lee and James Yimm Lee's Broadway school in Oakland, California. Bruce Lee's artistic skills are reflected in this colorful sign. This kwoon signage was the beginning of the creative design that would eventually become the logo representing his personal self-defense art. Now the world knows it simply as jeet kune do, or JKD. The yin-yang design is in red and gold.

■ The Oakland Jun Fan Gung Fu gang of Oakland, California. A group photograph taken in front of the garage of 3039 Monticello Avenue, where Bruce Lee and James Yimm Lee developed the foundation of what the world has come to know as jeet kune do.

■ Oakland student Hank Maguire shows his diploma and gung-fu uniform from the Oakland years.

■ George Lee (left, kneeling) with co-author Greglon Lee.

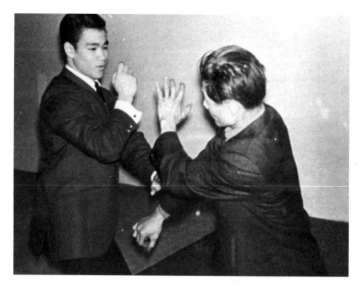

■ Bruce Lee (left) and James Yimm Lee demonstrating fighting techniques at Ralph Castro's Kenpo School in San Francisco, California.

■ James Yimm Lee (left) and Bruce Lee demonstrating fighting techniques at Ralph Castro's Kenpo School in San Francisco, California. Castro's dojo was one of the first commercial martial arts schools in the San Francisco area.

■ Bruce Lee (left foreground), James Yimm Lee (right foreground), Ed Parker (background left), and Ralph Castro (background right) at Castro's Kenpo School in San Francisco, California.

■ Bruce Lee and Ed Parker discussing the philosophies of Chinese gung-fu at Ralph Castro's Kenpo School in San Francisco, California.

■ A portrait of a young James Yimm Lee. He was in his early 20s when this photograph was taken in Oakland, California.

■ James Yimm Lee's birth certificate. He was born January 31, 1920.

■ James Yimm Lee in his U.S. Army uniform in 1945. James served in the Philippine Islands during World War II and contracted malaria there.

■ James Yimm Lee striking a fight pose. He was instrumental in sharing his knowledge of bodybuilding with Bruce Lee during the Oakland years.

■ James Yimm Lee's brothers and sisters. Left to right: Mabel (Lee) Chin, Helen (Lee) Lai, Jon Y. Lee, Robert Lee, Mamie (Lee) Fong, and Jennie (Lee) Lew.

■ Katherine Lee, the wife of James Yimm Lee. She succumbed to breast cancer complications.

■ James Yimm Lee.

■ Karena and Greglon Lee, James Yimm Lee's daughter and son.

■ Greglon Lee with sister Karena's friends at her birthday party in Oakland.

■ Celebrating James Yimm Lee's birthday in Oakland Chinatown. Allen Joe, Karena Lee, Greglon Lee, and Bruce Lee look on as James blows out the candles.

■ James Yimm Lee celebrates his birthday at Chinatown in Oakland, California. Bruce Lee shares this moment with James' family, students, and friends.

■ James Yimm Lee, Linda Emery Lee, and Bruce Lee.

■ Linda Lee and Bruce Lee with their baby son Brandon at Lake Merritt in Oakland, California. Bruce and Linda were living with James Yimm Lee and family during the time this shot was taken.

To Karen,

■ A signed publicity photograph to Karena Lee (James Lee's daughter) during his **Green Hornet** "Kato" days. It is signed, "To Karen, Love Bruce Lee."

■ James Lee (left) with Bruce Lee on the set of **The Green Hornet** television show. James' daughter Karena and son Greglon are in the foreground.

■ On the set of **The Green Hornet** television show. Left to right: Van Williams (who played Britt Reid), George Lee, and Bruce Lee (who played the role of Kato) (1966–1967).

■ On the set of **The Green Hornet** television show. Left to right: George Lee, Bruce Lee, Allen Joe, and James Yimm Lee.

James Lee, Master of Kung fu

Funeral services for James Yimm Lee, a leading exponent of the Wing Chun school of the Chinese martial art of kung-fu, will be at 2 p.m. tomorrow at the Albert Brown Mortuary in Oakland.

Mr. Lee died last Thurs. day at the age of 52.

Born in Oakland, Mr. Lee broke Northern California weight lifting records in 1938 for his class as a member of the Oakland YMCA, team. He was an amateur boxer a high school gymnast and wrestler and one of three kung-fu instructors to study under Survivors include daughter Karena Lee, two sons, Greglon Lee and Richard Jeong: two brothers, John and Robert Lee, and four sisters, Mrs. Helen Lai, Mrs. Mamie Chan, Mrs. Jennie Leu and Mrs. Mabel Chin.

■ James Yimm Lee's obituary as it appeared in the **Oakland Tribune** newspaper. He passed away on Thursday, December 28, 1972, at the young age of 52.

■ The resting place and headstone of James Yimm Lee at the Mountain View Cemetery (Plot 410) in Oakland, California. Notice the jeet kune do logo that reads "An Inspiration True Comrade of JKD."

■ Greglon Lee at his father's grave site at the Mountain View Cemetery in Oakland, California.

■ Felix Macias, Sr., at James Yimm Lee's grave site honoring his teacher.

■ James Yimm Lee's Certificate of Death. The established date of death is December 28, 1972. The filed date is December 30, 1972.

■ The press photo of Bruce Lee that was used worldwide with his obituary.

■ Bruce Lee's obituary as it appeared in Hong Kong on Friday, July 20, 1973. This newspaper article was run by the Associated Press and was in publications all over the world.

■ A rare photograph of Bruce Lee in a restaurant in Los Angeles, California.

Part Three

Part Three

Timeline of James Yimm Lee's Life

A Brief James Yimm Lee Biography

James Yimm Lee was the son of Lee Look On and Ching Shee Lee. His father Lee Look On was born in San Francisco in 1880 and during his adult years established himself as a merchant by trade. For a time, Lee Look On was the proprietor of a shrimp company on Harrison Street in Oakland Chinatown. He later became a tailor and even ran a prosperous gambling house. James Yimm Lee's mother, Ching Shee Lee, was born in China in 1880 and later immigrated to the United States and assumed the American name of Alice Lee.

The Lee family was blessed with three sons and five daughters: Jon Y. Lee, Robert Lee, James Yimm Lee, Helen (Lee) Lai, Mamie (Lee) Fong, Jennie (Lee) Lew, Mabel (Lee) Chin, and Gladys Lee, who died of polio while still a young girl.

1920, January 31—Oakland, Calif.: At 8:30 in the morning on January 31, 1920, Lee Kein Heir was born at his parents' house at 927 Webster Street in Oakland, California. Shortly afterward, an American name was adopted that included the original family surname. He was to be known as James Yimm Lee. Although Lee Kein Heir is recorded on James Yimm Lee's birth certificate, his father's real Chinese surname had been Yimm, but he had changed it to Lee for immigration purposes upon entering the United States. James always felt it proper to include his true surname when his American name was used.

1926, September 4 (Age 6)—Oakland, Calif.: James starts attending Lincoln School in Oakland Chinatown. He became school president two times by the 7th and 8th grades.

1928 (Age 8)—Oakland, Calif.: As a youth James was constantly ill. He started going to an herbalist to receive treatments and also started to do physical training to build up his body.

1930, September (Age 10)—Oakland, Calif.: By the age of 10, James was beginning to excel at sports and other physical activities sanctioned by his grade school. During this early time he also expressed an avid interest in physical development and even an interest in martial arts. James was quite close to his older brothers Jon and Robert. Jon Lee, the eldest of the brothers, was like a second father to James and he seemed to be the only one who could offer the discipline that young James, who was often mischievous, needed in those times.

1938, June (Age 18)—Oakland, Calif.: James became very preoccupied with physical fitness and weightlifting while still in his teens. At the age of 18, while still attending Oakland Technical High School, James Yimm Lee broke the Northern California weightlifting records in his weight class. At the time he was a member of the Oakland YMCA weightlifting team.

1939, January (Age 19)—Oakland, Calif.: By the time he graduated from Oakland Technical High School in January 1939, James had won many awards for his outstanding performances in gymnastics, wrestling, and even amateur boxing.

Despite his slight, 5'6" frame, his physique had developed quite nicely and was highly defined. For several years after graduation he was totally engrossed with physical fitness. Many of his friends and close buddies would call him nicknames such as "Shoulders" Lee, Lee the "Vee" man, or "Tiger" Lee because of his bold and confident attitude.

1940, March (Age 20)—Oakland, Calif.: By the time that James was 20, he was considered a rather tough kid around Oakland Chinatown. The confidence and physical abilities he had acquired through constant training prompted many of the people in Oakland Chinatown to refer to him as a real "roughneck" with a reputation for quickly defending his actions. This reputation occasionally required him to defend himself against individuals who did not see eye-to-eye with his attitudes.

1940, October (Age 20)—Vallejo, Calif.: James soon realized that if he was to survive he was going to need a profession that would gain him financial independence. At the age of 20, after being accepted as an apprentice welder at the Mare Island Naval Shipyards in Vallejo, California, he began in earnest to learn a trade that would be the mainstay of his occupational career. After working with naval ships and submarines for about one and one-half years and quickly learning the techniques of the welding trade, he began to feel the urge for travel and excitement.

1941, December 1 (Age 21)—Pearl Harbor, Hawai'i: James Yimm Lee put in for a transfer to Pearl Harbor, Hawai'i, and as a result arrived there on December 1, 1941, just six days before the Japanese bombed Pearl Harbor. So it was that at the young age of 21, James was plunged directly into the most devastating battle that ever raged in the Pacific. With the beginning of World War II in the Pacific theater, James, along with many other shipbuilders and welders, was immediately put to work before the final bombings had subsided.

For the next two and one-half years James and his co-workers worked tirelessly trying to help salvage what was left of the United States naval fleet. It was during this time, in his rare off-hours, that James began a serious interest in the study of martial arts.

1944 (Age 24)—Pearl Harbor, Hawai'i: Working in the shipyards for the war effort, James took up judo and iron-hand training. He and several of his fellow workers began to train in the arts of judo and jujitsu with the late Professor Okazaki at his martial arts gym in Honolulu. On occasions when they could not attend the classes at the school, Professor Okazaki would form special classes at the bus terminal near where James and his fellow students lived.

1944, June 20 (Age 24)—Oakland, Calif.: Early in June 1944, after two and one-half years of intermittent martial arts training and continual work to restore the salvaged ships, James Yimm Lee returned to Oakland to visit his family and friends.

1944, August 17 (Age 24)—U.S. Army, San Francisco, Calif.: Two months later, after being involved with the war firsthand in Pearl Harbor, he was inducted into the United States Army. In addition to James, his two brothers also joined to fight for their country.

1944, November 23 (Age 24)—U.S. Army, Fort Knox, Ky.: After a brief stint in basic training, James was stationed at Fort Knox, Kentucky, where he attended radio operator school.

1945, January 11 (Age 24)—U.S. Army, Philippine Islands: Upon completion of the necessary training he was attached to the 716th Tank Battalion in the Philippine Islands, where he was stationed for about a year. During his tour of duty in the Philippines, James Yimm Lee saw plenty of action and was in combat against the Japanese at the Luzon Campaign. He performed several functions during these combat periods. He was primarily a radio operator stationed with the tank battalion but out of necessity to survive the forceful attacks by the Japanese, he also became a machine gunner. James was also engaged in the Mindanao Campaign, for which he received the Asiatic Pacific Theater Ribbon with two Bronze Stars, the Philippine Liberation Ribbon, and the World War II Victory Medal.

During the fierce combative encounters, James was lucky that he was never wounded while in action but he contracted the dreaded malaria disease during the latter part of the Philippine Campaign. Before the close of the war, he had severe reoccurring bouts with this tropical fever, which weakened his physical condition considerably. In several of the bouts he nearly died due to the intense heat and climate of the South Pacific.

1946, January 10 (Age 25)—Letterman Hospital (U.S. Army), San Francisco, Calif.: On January 10, 1946, he departed the Philippines for intense medical supervision and eight days later he was registered at the Letterman General Hospital in San Francisco, California. After three months of treatment and medical attention, James was released from the United States Army with an honorable discharge and a 30% medical disability. After seeing action in the South Pacific for the duration of the war he was awarded the rank of Private First Class while assigned to the 801st Military Police Battalion of San Francisco, California.

1946, April 22 (Age 26)—Oakland, Calif.: James Yimm Lee returned to Oakland, California. For the next five years he lived at his parents' home on 321 Perkins Street in Oakland. During this interim period, James resumed his weight training and bodybuilding to restore his health, and took up a civilian occupation as an electrical welder for a local firm. Remaining a confirmed bachelor, bound and determined to get in the best physical shape of his life, he pursued bodybuilding and martial arts with a renewed interest.

During those intense five years, he and many of his close associates and friends from before the war began to work out and train regularly at many of the physical fitness clubs in the Oakland area. This was a very formative time in James' life.

1948 (Age 28)—Berkeley, Calif.: Changing jobs, James began working at Universal Window as a welder.

1951, October 13 (Age 31)—Washoe County, Nev.: James married Katherine Margaret Chow in Washoe County, Nevada, and moved to 14th Avenue in Oakland. James met 28-year-old Katherine while attending a dinner party given by one of his close friends.

Katherine was raised in San Jose, California, and was one of three daughters of Fannie Chow, a widow. Her sisters were Rebecca (Chow) Eastman and Esther (Chow) Louie. The Chow family had grown up on a farm in San Jose, and Katherine had attended San Jose State College for two years but never graduated. For income, she worked as a waitress, a Chinese cook, and a clerk-typist for the federal government and later at the Naval Air Station in Alameda, California. Before James, Katherine had been married twice and had one son, Richard Jeong.

1952, May 27 (Age 32)—Oakland, Calif.: James and Katherine had a baby daughter named Karena Beverly Lee.

1953, October 31 (Halloween Day) (Age 33)—Oakland, Calif.: James and Katherine had a baby son named Greglon Yimm Lee. Greglon's unusual name was a combination of the names of James' two favorite actors, Gregory Peck and Marlon Brando.

1955, June 20 (Age 35)—Oakland, Calif.: James Yimm Lee's family moved to a larger house located at 584 Valle Vista Avenue in Oakland, California.

1956, August (Age 36)—Oakland, Calif.: James began writing his own martial arts manuals.

1957 (Age 37)—Oakland, Calif.: James began general research into the publishing business.

1957, June (Age 37)—San Francisco, Calif.: By late June, while the children were growing up, James Yimm Lee's interest in the Chinese (gung-fu) forms of martial arts had intensified. He began training in San Francisco Chinatown under the tutelage of Professor T.Y. Wong, a noted authority in the sil lum art of Chinese gung-fu. This proved to be a very rewarding experience for James, and he spent about three and one-half years pursuing the ancient sil lum methods of self-defense taught by Professor Wong at his respectable kwoon (school) in Chinatown (the Kin Mon Chinese Institute on Waverly Place in San Francisco Chinatown).

1957, July (Age 37)—Oakland, Calif.: James Yimm Lee's martial arts was beginning to blossom through several outlets. He had become involved with operating a weightlifting gym, began to demonstrate his physical martial arts skills both in traditional techniques and in martial arts weapon practice, began writing and publishing martial arts books, as well as incorporating his welding skills to produce unique training apparatus and equipment that would enhance the practitioners' overall fighting capabilities.

He began a writing career that produced such books as *Fighting Arts of the Orient: Elemental Karate and Kung-Fu* and *Modern Kung-Fu Karate: Iron Poison Hand Training,* in which he demonstrated and taught the proper training methods for developing strong, uncalloused hands that could break large stacks of solid bricks without causing injury to the hands, and how to construct one's own training equipment to develop and strengthen one's hands and feet for self-defense purposes. A layman with only 100 days of proper training could perform many of the breaking techniques taught within his books.

1958, January (Age 38)—Oakland, Calif.: James Lee's creative talents extended into the mail-order book business. He started Oriental Book Sales publishing company. From this home-based company he published, promoted, distributed, and sold his own publications, as well as those of several other popular martial arts authors of the time. He was instrumental in supplying the guidance and advice for other aspiring martial artists who wished to publish their creative works.

1959, August 2 (Age 39)—Oakland, Calif.: The James Lee family moved again, to 3039 Monticello Avenue in Oakland, a bigger house with a spacious garage in which to train martial arts. James began accepting private students.

1959, October (Age 39)—Oakland, Calif.: By 1959, word had traveled far and wide that James Lee was one of the most knowledgeable martial artists in the United States, and many serious practitioners sought him out for instruction and advice. He was often an invited guest at different functions and was always urged to perform his incredible breaking feats. These techniques were so unbelievable that most people doubted their validity until they had attempted them themselves.

His knowledge of the laws of physics was so advanced that he could stack a pile of solid house bricks and then announce which one in the stack he would break. James had acquired a tremendous amount of physical power for his small frame and could direct that power with a very high degree of accuracy and control.

1960 (Age 40)—Oakland, Calif.: James published two books, one of his own and one by Professor T.Y. Wong.

1960 (Age 40)—San Francisco, Calif.: James Yimm Lee met Bruce Lee at a cha-cha class in San Francisco and began training and sharing martial arts knowledge with him, terminating his training with Professor T.Y. Wong.

1961 (Age 41)—Oakland, Calif.: James often hosted Bruce Lee as a guest at his house during Bruce's trips from Seattle to Oakland. Meeting of the martial arts "gang" began in Oakland; its members were Bruce, James, Allen Joe, Al Novak, Ralph Castro, George Lee, and others.

1962 (Age 42)—Oakland, Calif.: Bruce continued to visit James periodically as his studies at the University of Washington in Seattle and his gung-fu class schedule permitted.

1963 (Age 43)—Oakland, Calif.: James helped Bruce publish his first book *Chinese Gung-Fu: The Philosophical Art of Self-Defense.*

1964, August 2 (Age 44)—Long Beach, Calif.: James suggested to Ed Parker that the "Chinese gung-fu man" Bruce Lee demonstrate at Ed Parker's International Karate Championships in Long Beach, California. Ed took the suggestion and had Bruce Lee as a guest and performer at his event.

1964, October 5 (Age 44)—Oakland, Calif.: James' wife Katherine died. Soon afterward, Bruce and Linda Lee moved into James' home to help take care of the children. James and Bruce opened a commercial studio at 42nd and Broadway. The famous challenge between Bruce and Wong Jack Man takes place at the studio. After six months, James and Bruce decided to close the studio and teach out of his Monticello Avenue home.

1965 (Age 45)—Oakland, Calif.: Bruce, Linda, and Brandon Lee moved to Los Angeles.

1971 (Age 51)—Oakland, Calif.: James was told he had inoperable lung cancer, but still continued to train.

1972, December 28 (Age 52)—Oakland, Calif.: James Yimm Lee died. A funeral ceremony was held in Oakland and was attended by his many friends and fans. Prior to James' death, his wing chun book was published with Ohara Publications (*Black Belt* magazine). Bruce Lee served as technical editor and, using the influence born from his Hollywood successes, helped ensure that this final book was published before James' death, bringing full circle the publication cycle, which started with James' publication of Bruce's first book.

Timeline of Bruce Lee's Life

A Brief Bruce Lee Biography

Bruce Lee's father, Lee Hoi Cheun, was born around the turn of the century in Fatshan Province, China. His mother, Grace Oi Yue Lee, was born in Shanghai in 1912. She was Eurasian, born to a German Catholic father and Chinese mother. Bruce's father was a comic actor in classical Chinese opera and in 1940, his pregnant wife and three children, Peter, Agnes Chan (adopted), and Phoebe Ho, accompanied him on a tour of the United States. During the tour Grace, who had suffered a miscarriage only thirteen months previously, elected to remain in San Francisco to await the birth of her third natural child.

1940, November 27—San Francisco, Calif.: Bruce Lee (Lee Jun Fan) was born in the Year of the Dragon between 6 and 8 a.m. (the Hour of the Dragon) at the Jackson Street Memorial Hospital in San Francisco's Chinatown. At the time of Bruce's birth, his father was performing with the Cantonese Opera Company 3,000 miles away in New York. Grace called the boy "Jun Fan," which translates as "return again," meaning that Bruce would one day return to the city of his birth. The English spelling of Lee was used for convenience on the U.S. birth certificate, and the English name "Bruce" was provided by Dr. Mary Glover, the doctor who attended his delivery. The Lee family remained in San Francisco for some time following the birth.

At three months old, Bruce debuted as a "prop baby" in the film *Golden Gate Girl* in San Francisco, California. He played the role of a baby girl carried by his father. This was to be the first of eighteen film roles as a child actor, including *Kid Cheung, Thunderstorm, In the Face of Demolition,* and *The Orphan.* The popularity he enjoyed with local audiences led them to nickname him "Little Dragon," a name that would be revived to great effect when he later enjoyed international movie success.

1941 (Age 1)—Hong Kong: Bruce and his parents returned to their family home in Kowloon, which was an apartment at 218 Nathan Road, Kowloon District. The apartment was located on the second story of a building that contained a store on the ground level. These early years were far from trouble-free for the young Bruce, who was a frail child. The earlier miscarriage of Grace's second son caused the family to bow to Chinese superstition and rename baby Bruce as a girl to confuse evil spirits; so Bruce became known to his family as "Sai-Fun," which means "little phoenix," the phoenix being the female equivalent of the dragon.

1946 (Age 5)—Hong Kong: While accompanying his father to the set of a Hong Kong produced movie he was acting in, Bruce was given an opportunity to appear in the movie *The Beginning of a Boy.* Later that year, he performed in *The Birth of Mankind* and *My Son, Ah Cheung.* It was during these formative years that Bruce, being nearsighted, began wearing prescription glasses, something he would hate throughout his teenage years. It was not until he returned to the United States that he would correct this plaguing problem by wearing contact lenses, suggested to him by friend and student Ernie Benevidez, who was an optometrist in Oakland, California.

1952 (Age 11)—Hong Kong: Bruce began attending La Salle College, an all-boys' school. As his tutor Brother Henry Pang recalled, Bruce resented authority, so this was not to be the happy association his parents had hoped for. Bruce was eventually asked to leave for locking a school bully in a toilet cubicle overnight. (Bruce, after achieving film star status, returned in 1973 to receive a special honorable school award from the faculty.) Bruce's parents then enrolled him in St. Francis Xavier College, a Catholic high school, hoping he would fare better.

1953 (Age 13)—Hong Kong: During his birthday party at his family's Nathan Road apartment, Bruce met William Cheung, who was a young martial artist attending the wing chun school of Grandmaster Yip Man. A rapport quickly developed between the two boys, and Bruce pestered his mother for the HK$12 (12 Hong Kong dollar) fee per lesson to attend the gung-fu class in Yaumati District. Bruce having been recently beaten up by a street gang and claiming "bullying" at school, Grace capitulated (although it was Bruce who did most of the bullying). Bruce and William also tagged along with a local street gang, the Junction Street 8 Tigers, one of many such gangs that were prevalent in Hong Kong at the time.

1954 (Age 13)—Hong Kong: While still developing his wing chun skills, Bruce decided to take up cha-cha dancing, mainly for the potential to meet and impress girls. Also during this time, perhaps due to Bruce's fascination with movie icon James Dean, Bruce's "rebel image" began to emerge; pictures of Bruce around this era depict him with greased hair and denims.

1955 (Age 14)—Hong Kong: Bruce Lee's prowess in the martial art of wing chun was becoming apparent to all who knew him. Often, he would arrive at wing chun class fifteen minutes early and tell other students that class was canceled that day. This enabled him to gain personal instruction from a puzzled Yip Man or his senior instructor, Wong Sheung Leung.

1958 (Age 17)—Hong Kong: Bruce was noticed as a "hot prospect" by Brother Edward, the boxing coach at St. Francis Xavier. Entering the inter-school boxing match against rival school King George V, Bruce blasted his way through three preliminary rounds before coming up against the champion of the previous year, Gary Elms. Bruce's "straight-blasting" wing chun punching confounded his opponent, and Bruce was declared 1958 high school boxing champion. Boosting his confidence even more was his win in the Crown Colony Cha-Cha Championship with his partner, Miss (Pearl) Cho Miu Yee. He and Pearl became the cha-cha champions of Hong Kong in 1958. Bruce even carried a card with as many as 120 dance steps on it in his wallet! To make his situation even more envious, he also landed a leading role in the film *The Orphan*, which was the last movie he made as a child actor. It was also the only movie in which Bruce did not fight.

1959 (Age 18)—Hong Kong: Jealousy, rivalry, and Bruce's cockiness led him to be involved in numerous street fights, some reaching such a severe level that it caused police involvement. In early 1959, rivals from another gung-fu school of the *Choy Li Fut* style challenged Bruce to a friendly "match." These matches usually occurred on rooftops to avoid attracting attention in crowded Hong Kong. Wong Sheung Leung, Bruce's senior in wing chun, refereed the bout, which was an uneventful affair until a rival struck Bruce in the eye, cutting it badly. Bruce retaliated by wildly battering his opponent against the rooftop water tank. The police were summoned and a subdued Bruce was brought before his mother, who was coerced by the police into signing a paper stating she would keep Bruce out of further trouble. Sure that Bruce would soon return to his wild ways, Bruce's parents decided that he should be sent to the United States. Their thinking was that such a trip would be a possible means to get him back on the right track by allowing Bruce to return to the land of his birth and register for the U.S. draft before his 19th birthday, thereby claiming his American citizenship. Bruce readily seized the opportunity to return to his birthplace of San Francisco and of a new beginning in a new country. As time was running out for him to claim his American citizenship, in April, Bruce boarded a ship of the American President Lines for the eighteen-day transpacific crossing, traveling third class.

1959, May 17 (Age 18)—San Francisco, Calif.: With $15 from his father and $100 from his mother, Bruce Lee arrived in San Francisco, California, accompanied by his brother Peter, and was met by his sister Agnes. Quan Ging Ho, an old friend of his father's, provided him with a place to stay. He earned his keep by working odd jobs in the various Chinese communities and by giving cha-cha and gung-fu lessons to anyone who would employ him. While attending a housewarming, Bruce was introduced to Robert Lee (no relation), who was the elder brother of a gung-fu practitioner named James Yimm Lee. James had studied sil lum gung-fu under Professor T.Y. Wong at his Waverly Place kwoon in San Francisco,

California. James, having heard that Bruce was a top gung-fu stylist, tried to get in touch but Bruce was unfortunately moving to Seattle with his brother, so the two were unable to meet. Before moving to Seattle Bruce visited the Manhattan District in New York City and met Master Gin Foon Mark, a praying mantis gung-fu man who taught in New York's Chinatown.

1959, September 3 (Age 18)—Seattle, Wash.: Bruce completed his relocation to Seattle and secured an attic room from Lee family friend Ruby Chow, located above her restaurant. Ruby Chow was a well-respected and civic-minded Seattle matriarch who had run a successful restaurant business for years. The arrangement she had made with Bruce's parents was that he would be employed as a waiter and busboy while he attended school in Seattle. Bruce enrolled in the local college, Edison Technical School, and was determined to make a good start in his new life, eventually earning his high school diploma. However, Bruce didn't care for the menial job and his lowly position at the restaurant and it soon became apparent to most of the regular patrons that Ruby Chow and Bruce had an intense dislike for one another.

School studies during the day and restaurant work at night was a little more than he chose to accept, so as a way to make some money and free himself from the depressing work conditions at Ruby Chow's Restaurant, he quickly assimilated into the local Chinese community and began to introduce his wing chun gung-fu at such places as backyards and city parks. He also gave a gung-fu demonstration at the 1959 Seattle "Seafair" exhibition. One person who was impressed by Bruce's demonstration and his ballet-like grace was judo expert Jesse Glover, who persuaded Bruce to teach him. Their first informal training hall was the corner of Maynard and Lane and moved to the parking lot of the Blue Cross Hospital building as Bruce's students increased. This was the most informal teaching period of Bruce Lee's martial arts career; never again would he be as "open" with his knowledge of gung-fu. Around this time, Bruce dated his first girlfriend in the United States, Japanese-American Amy Sanbo.

Soon, a number of students were training under Bruce Lee. One, a Japanese-American named Taky Kimura, eighteen years Bruce's senior, became a devoted follower. Although Taky was not as physically gifted as other students from this era, such as Roy Hollingsworth, Bruce sensed an inner strength in Taky. He soon became Bruce's right-hand man in Seattle, replacing original student Jesse Glover, who was somewhat disappointed by this transition. Jesse gradually withdrew from training with the group, but he would remain on friendly terms with Bruce for the remainder of his life.

1961 (Age 20)—Seattle, Wash.: In early 1961, Bruce's growing reputation led him and fellow martial artist Fook Young into giving a televised demonstration of sil lum and wing chun forms for Seattle's local TV station.

1961, March 27 (Age 20)—Seattle, Wash.: Bruce enrolled at the University of Washington, studying philosophy and teaching gung-fu to students at school. When his first informal gung-fu school housed in a dingy basement laundry room was closed, he opened another on the university campus district. It was nearer his place of study and better placed to gain the interest of passing university students.

1962 (Age 21)—Oakland, Calif.: Having heard of James Yimm Lee, Bruce drove to the Bay Area to meet him. This heralds the **BEGINNING OF THE OAKLAND YEARS (1962–1965).** Bruce visited

James at his home in Oakland, California, and their mutual obsession with gung-fu led to an immediate rapport. James, who self-published his own martial arts training guides, would later publish Bruce Lee's first book, titled *Chinese Gung-Fu: The Philosophical Art of Self-Defense*. The photographs for the book would be taken, at James Yimm Lee's request, in the parking lot behind Ruby Chow's Restaurant. Because of Bruce's very limited budget, the book would have an initial print run of only 1,500 copies. Bruce now began to see the fruits of a possible collaboration with James and began to discuss opening a second branch of the Jun Fan Gung Fu Institute (the name he now used for his kwoons) in Oakland.

1963, Summer (Age 22)—Hong Kong: Bruce returned to Hong Kong with friend Doug Palmer to visit family for the first time since he had moved to the U.S. Also during this visit, Bruce's father insisted that Bruce be circumcised; Bruce reluctantly complied and after the operation, walked bowlegged for a couple of days.

At the end of the summer and upon his return to Seattle, he found his draft papers waiting. He went to the Induction Center but was amazed to find himself rejected by the U.S. Army, classified as "4F" due to an apparently undescended testicle, poor eyesight, and a sinus disorder. Bruce was somewhat bemused to be the fittest man the Army ever rejected; however, he did eventually don a uniform as a member of the campus ROTC squad.

1963, October 25 (Age 22)—Seattle, Wash.: Having given notice to Ruby Chow, Bruce opened a formal Jun Fan Gung Fu Institute and attracted students by inserting ads into the Sunday edition of the *Seattle Times*. This initial publicity would prove to be very valuable as Bruce began expanding and teaching his art to the curious Westerners. He also promoted himself and gained interest for his school by giving martial arts demonstrations and teaching basic self-defense at any place he could.

One such place was at Garfield High School; it was here that Bruce first demonstrated the "one-inch punch" to an amazed audience. This is the punch, which he and James DeMille had developed in Seattle. that he would later make famous at the 1964 Long Beach Internationals. Among the audience at Garfield was 17-year-old Linda Emery, an American of Swedish descent. Bruce soon began to take an interest in the attractive blonde, and they enjoyed their first date on October 25, 1963, at the revolving restaurant atop the Seattle Space Needle, a landmark built for the 1962 Seattle World's Fair. Bruce and Linda's relationship quickly became more intense. She realized that Bruce had some big plans and an exciting destiny... and decided to join him on the journey.

1963, Fall (Age 22)—Seattle, Wash.: Bruce moved his Jun Fan Gung Fu Institute to 4750 University Way, a building near the university campus. He taught any person of any race at a time when most Asian martial arts schools would teach only people of their own race.

1964 (Age 23)—Oakland, Calif.: Bruce continued to discuss plans to open a second Jun Fan Gung Fu Institute in Oakland, California, with James Yimm Lee. He and James also discussed many aspects of the fighting arts, and Bruce began to incorporate other systems, such as judo, which he learned under the tutelage of Master Shuzo Kato, and trained with his friend Fred Sato.

His collaboration with James Lee developed rapidly and in January 1964, James introduced Bruce to karate luminary Ed Parker, who often instructed celebrities such as Elvis Presley and Frank Sinatra. (Ed Parker has been credited in the U.S. as the father of modern day kenpo-karate in the United States.) Through James and Ed, Bruce also met Wally Jay and on May 2, Bruce gave a demonstration for Wally's Judo Jujitsu Club at their luau in Alameda, California.

1964, Summer (Age 23)—Oakland, Calif.: By July 19, 1964, Bruce had decided that his destiny lay in moving to California. At the end of the summer semester he abandoned his university philosophy course, just three units short of graduating. His campus Jun Fan Gung Fu Institute was returned to the humble laundry basement it had started in, under the permanent leadership of Taky Kimura. A nervous Linda Emery drove Bruce Lee to the airport and kissed him farewell as he left for his new start in Oakland, with his promise "I'll be back for you..." ringing in her ears. Once in Oakland, plans were finalized with James Yimm Lee to open a Jun Fan Kung Fu Institute there.

1964, August (Age 23)—Washington, D.C.: Bruce met Jhoon Rhee at the International Karate Championships. The two would remain good friends and Jhoon Rhee would later invite Bruce to Washington, D.C., to appear at tournaments.

1964, August 2 (Age 23)—Long Beach, Calif.: Ed Parker, known as the father of American karate (kenpo), invited Bruce to give a demonstration at his 1964 International Karate Championships tournament. It was here where Bruce performed a variety of incredible physical feats, including his two-finger push-ups. He executed some extremely fast back-fist strikes that were virtually impossible for the audience to see, and once he saw that the audience was duly impressed, he used his and James Lee's Oakland student Robert (Bob) Baker to demonstrate his "one-inch" punch. The incredible punch knocked Bob back about five feet into a chair, which then slid back another five or so feet, all of which was being filmed by Ed Parker's camera crew. Unbeknownst to Bruce Lee, his life was about to change in a very radical sense.

1964, August 12 (Age 23)—Seattle, Wash.: Bruce returned to Seattle to propose to and marry Linda Emery, despite significant protest from her mother, Vivian, and stepfather, Willard Dickinson, over her intention to marry a "Chinese boy" who didn't have a job. However, following Linda's announcement that she was pregnant, common sense prevailed.

1964, August 17 (Age 23)—Seattle, Wash.: Bruce Lee married Linda Emery at the Seattle Congregational Church, using a wedding ring borrowed from James Lee's wife Katherine. Taky Kimura was his best man. Soon afterward, they moved to Oakland and began living with James Yimm Lee's family at their home on Monticello Avenue.

1964, October 5 (Age 23)—Oakland, Calif.: James Lee's wife Katherine passed away due to complications from breast cancer.

1965 (Age 24)—Oakland, Calif.: Several months after he began teaching, Bruce was challenged by Wong Jack Man, a leading gung-fu practitioner in the Chinatown community. They agreed that if Bruce lost, he would either close his school or stop teaching Caucasians; if Jack lost, he would stop teaching. Wong Jack Man did not believe Bruce would actually fight and attempted to delay the match, but Bruce became angered and insisted that they not wait. Wong then tried to put limitations on techniques; Bruce refused "rules" and the two fought no-holds-barred. In the first few minutes of what could only be described as an uncontrollable "street fight," neither fighter could claim a decisive victory. Wong's tactic of turning his back every time Bruce attempted to hit him (and Bruce's seeming inability to counter this tactic) made for an unseemly spectacle, but Bruce began to prevail. Students of Wong attempted to step in and help their Sifu, but James was able to prevent it. Bruce eventually sent Wong and his students packing, but would admit to James Lee, "That was the strangest fight I've ever been in; that guy kept circling, and I couldn't get a good shot. I hurt my hands hitting him in the back of the head!"

Later, bothered as to why the fight took so long, he began to reevaluate his style and came to the conclusion that he was not in his top physical condition. He began watching Western boxing matches on film while James was at work and Linda attended to the household duties and the care of Karena and Greglon. James and Bruce also traveled to local bookstores in Oakland, Berkeley, and the surrounding neighborhood communities in search of books on boxing, fencing, savate (French foot fighting), and any other reference sources that would enable him to incorporate footwork, artful strategies, and variation into his training. At the Monticello Avenue home, he would spend time during the day conditioning himself and achieved the ability to run six miles daily to increase his stamina. Thus, with James Lee's help and supportive martial arts contributions, the early concepts of jeet kune do (JKD), The Way of the Intercepting Fist, were developed.

Shortly after the Wong match, Jay Sebring (a hairdresser who had witnessed Bruce's Long Beach triumph) happened to mention the "amazing Chinese guy" to *Batman* and *Perry Mason* TV producer William Dozier, who was coincidentally on the lookout for a young Chinese actor to play Charlie Chan's son in an upcoming TV series called *Number One Son*. Dozier telephoned Ed Parker to ask about Bruce. Ed showed him the original 16mm movie footage he had filmed of Bruce's Long Beach demonstration. Dozier was sufficiently impressed that he called Bruce in Oakland to arrange an immediate screen test.

1965, February 1 (Age 24)—Oakland, Calif.: Linda gave birth to their first child, marking a dramatic turn in Bruce Lee's life. The baby, a son, was named Brandon Bruce Lee and became the newest arrival at James Yimm Lee's home on Monticello Avenue.

1965, February 4 (Age 24)—Hollywood, Calif.: Bruce traveled to the 20th Century Fox studio in Hollywood for his first-ever screen test. The screen test was very successful and Bruce was signed to a one-year option for the *Number One Son* title role, receiving an $1,800 retainer fee.

1965, February 8 (Age 24)—Hong Kong: Bruce's father passed away in Hong Kong and Bruce returned for his father's funeral. At the funeral home, as dictated by Chinese tradition, in order to obtain forgiveness for not being present at his father's death, Bruce crawled on his knees toward the casket, wailing loudly and crying.

1965, May (Age 24)—Hong Kong: Bruce used the retainer money from the *Number One Son* to fly himself, Linda, and Brandon back to Hong Kong in order to settle his father's estate and to show their new baby to his mother and family. While there, Bruce used the opportunity to take pictures of Yip Man and other wing chun clan members to aid in the research for a gung-fu book he was working on with James back in Oakland, California. He also took Brandon to see Yip Man in hope of trying to persuade Yip Man to perform on 8mm home movie film. Bruce wanted to take the footage back to Seattle and Oakland to show James Lee and his other students what the man looked like in action. Yip Man modestly declined because he did not wish to release this knowledge for public display or to outside knowledge seekers, preferring to keep his training and special techniques within his kwoon.

Records also show that Bruce trained at the Hong Kong Hak Keny gym on May 27.

1965, September (Age 24)—Seattle, Wash.: Bruce, Linda, and Brandon return to Seattle, staying with Linda's family and proudly showing off their new son Brandon. While there, Bruce received word that the *Number One Son* project was canceled, disappointing both him and Linda. Linda threw him a birthday party to raise his spirits.

1965, December (Age 25)—Oakland, Calif.: After Christmas, the Bruce Lee family returned to James Lee's home in Oakland. Bruce received a call from the Greenway production studio, informing him that William Dozier had proposed a new series in a similar vein to the spoof action show *Batman* and it had been approved. This series was *The Green Hornet*, due for production in March 1966.

(*The Green Hornet* was originally created for a 1930s radio series by George Trendle. For the 1966 TV version, the original Filipino chauffeur was changed to the role of Kato, Japanese chauffeur and sidekick to millionaire newspaper publisher Britt Reid, who is the grandson of the Lone Ranger. This partly explains why Reid became by night a crime-fighting vigilante in a green overcoat and Lone Ranger style mask. The show ran for twenty-six half-hour episodes.)

1966, March 4 (Age 25)—Oakland, Calif.: Bruce Lee received a first-draft script from writer Lorenzo Semple, Jr. He then traveled to

Los Angeles and filmed a second screen test for Dozier, this time in full Kato-style costume and makeup. In the screen test, the actor playing the Green Hornet/Britt Reid character is apparently not Van Williams, and Bruce spoke only a few inconsequential lines. Thankfully, Dozier was not sufficiently discouraged to abandon *The Green Hornet* project.

1966, March 21 (Age 25)—Los Angeles, Calif.: Bruce Lee's TV career beckoned, so the Lee family bade a sad farewell to Oakland and their friend and benefactor James Yimm Lee and moved to an apartment on Wilshire and Gayley in the Los Angeles district of Westwood. Dozier once again screen-tested Bruce Lee for the *Green Hornet* role. In this second screen test, Bruce performed no gungfu and wore a different mask than was later developed for his role as "Kato."

The Green Hornet series started filming and Bruce was paid $400 per episode. It would later become known that Bruce had gotten the part of Kato because he was the only person who could accurately pronounce the star's name, Britt Reid.

1966, April 25 (Age 25)—Hollywood, Calif.: Bruce received a full script for the episode "Beautiful Dreamer" so he could study his acting lines. From production notes, this was not the premiere episode filmed, which was planned to be "The Ray Is for Killing." With the juxtaposition of the serials, the actual episode that premiered on TV was "The Silent Gun."

1966, August (Age 25)—Los Angeles, Calif.: The security of the role allowed the family to move into the plush Barrington Plaza condominium complex, which housed celebrities such as Burt Ward (Robin from the rival *Batman* show). Rumored rivalry between the actors was hyped up. In fact, Bruce gave Ward a quick gung-fu lesson.

1966, September 9 (Age 25)—Los Angeles, Calif.: *The Green Hornet* series premiered on TV. On September 28, Bruce Lee as "Kato" and Van Williams as the "Green Hornet" made a guest appearance on an episode of *Batman* entitled "The Spell of Tut." In the cameo, while the "caped crusaders" Batman (Adam West) and Robin (Burt Ward) are climbing the exterior of a skyscraper, the Green Hornet and Kato (Van Williams and Bruce Lee) emerge from a nearby window and exchange pleasantries. The result was a neat introduction of the newest Greenway Productions stars by producer Bill Dozier.

Bruce was a fabulous hit with children and adults alike. The audience had never seen anything like his gung-fu on screen before. Karena Beverly Lee (James Yimm Lee's daughter and godchild to Bruce and Linda Lee) became "Uncle Bruce's" unofficial "Kato" fan club president back in Oakland, California. In Hong Kong, *The Green Hornet* would become known as *The Kato Show*. The television series would also herald the first use of Bruce Lee's "signature" weapon—the nunchaku. One episode, "Praying Mantis," also featured his Los Angeles student Dan Inosanto. This episode featured Chinese character actor Mako as "Low Sing"; Dan doubled for Mako in his fight scenes with Bruce. One spectacular fight featured a variety of Kali (Filipino) weapons introduced to Bruce Lee by Inosanto.

1967, February 5 (Age 26)—Los Angeles Chinatown, Calif.: Bruce opened a "private" Gung Fu School at 628 College Street in Los Angeles Chinatown; entry was by invitation only. Some of his better-known students included Ted Wong, Dan Lee, Jerry Poteet, Richard Bustillo, Herb Jackson, Larry Hartsell, Bob Bremer, Pete

Jacobs, and Steve Golden. Prior to opening this school, Bruce had been privately training Tony Hum and Dan Inosanto at the rear of Wayne Chan's Pharmacy in Los Angeles. The friendship that blossomed between Bruce and Dan Inosanto and the personal gung-fu training that Bruce had given Dan prompted Bruce to recruit Dan as "Assistant Instructor" of the Los Angeles kwoon (school). This appointment was necessary due to Bruce's many publicity engagements and filming commitments. Eventually, when Bruce left for Hong Kong, he left Dan solely in charge of his "legacy" (with two exceptions: Taky Kimura ran his branch kwoon in Seattle and James Yimm Lee ran the operation in Oakland, California).

1967, May 6 (Age 26)—Washington, D.C.: Bruce Lee was a special guest, along with TV's *I Spy* star Robert Culp, at a Jhoon Rhee tournament at the Washington, D.C., Armory. While staying at the Mayflower Hotel, Bruce met his future friend and student, top karate man Joe Lewis. Lewis would later credit Bruce Lee's influence for his tournament wins.

1967, June 24 (Age 26)—New York City, N.Y.: Invited as a special celebrity guest, Bruce Lee attended Sihak Henry Cho's Tae Kwon Do Karate Championships, held in Madison Square Garden in New York City. He made personal appearances in full Kato mask and uniform, as he sometimes did following his fame with the Kato role. This appearance led to his meeting with karate champion Chuck Norris, among other notable competitors on the tournament circuit. This meeting would lead to Chuck training with Bruce. After Chuck had defeated Joe Lewis, Bruce presented him with his trophy as World Karate Champion.

1967, July 14 (Age 26)—Los Angeles, Calif.: In an episode of Raymond Burr's *Ironside* series (called *A Man Called Ironside* in the U.K.),

Bruce made a guest appearance as karate instructor Leon Soo. The episode was "Tagged for Murder." This was also the day the last episode of *The Green Hornet* television series aired. The series was later said to have failed because Bruce, playing a minor role as "Kato," became more popular than the main character Britt Reid (Van Williams).

The day following the cancellation of *The Green Hornet*, Bruce, Linda, and Brandon were forced to move out of the high-rent Barrington Plaza condominium, moving to a home in Inglewood in Southern California. Bruce was a regular lunch guest at 20th Century Fox of Charles Fitsimmons, Dozier's assistant on *The Green Hornet*, who suggested that, to sustain his lifestyle and newfound fame, Bruce should consider raising his present kwoon fee of $22 per month to the then-staggering fee of $50 per hour to teach celebrities. Bruce was astounded by the idea, but agreed to try it because he felt his time and professional experience as a teacher and actor would warrant that increase. Shortly afterward, Jay Sebring, now Bruce's barber, introduced him to Steve McQueen. In turn, this led to a longtime friendship with James Coburn. Stirling Silliphant (writer of *In the Heat of the Night* and *The Poseidon Adventure*) followed, as did Roman Polanski, James Garner, Lee Marvin, and Kareem Abdul-Jabbar, among others. Soon a steady flow of Hollywood stars were asking to train with Bruce Lee, who would eventually command an incredible $250 per hour!

1967, July 30 (Age 26)—Long Beach, Calif.: Bruce made his second appearance at Ed Parker's International Karate Championships in Long Beach, California. Despite the other martial arts luminaries on the bill, it was Bruce Lee's fame as Kato that drew the huge crowd to the event and evoked the greatest response. This audience witnessed Bruce's legendary "one-inch punch," and he performed push-ups on only *one* finger! Once again, the performance was filmed by the karate tournament promoter Ed Parker.

1967, November 4 (Age 26)—Alameda, Calif.: Bruce, as a favor to his friend Wally Jay, attended Wally's Alameda Island Judo Jujitsu Club as a celebrity guest. Around this time, a famous *Black Belt* magazine article appeared, with pictures taken at the Los Angeles Chinatown kwoon, entitled "In Kato's Gung fu, Action is Instant."

In late 1967 or early 1968, Bruce began some serious training sessions with martial arts star Chuck Norris. By March, he had begun teaching his celebrity students in earnest. These were the "lean" years of Bruce Lee's career, as acting roles for Asians were not readily available.

1968, July 5 (Age 27)—Hollywood, Calif.: Bruce earned a much-needed paycheck by choreographing fight scenes for the movie *The Wrecking Crew*, starring Dean Martin (as Matt Helm) and Sharon Tate (her last film before her murder). This was also Chuck Norris' movie debut and featured an adolescent Jackie Chan, as well as the celebrated Asian actress Nancy Kwan, famous for her starring role in the 1960 movie *The World of Suzie Wong*. (She would later play Seattle matriarch Ruby Chow in the 1993 Bruce Lee movie biography *Dragon: The Bruce Lee Story*.)

1968, August 6 (Age 27)—Hollywood, Calif.: Bruce played a cameo role in the film *Marlowe*, starring James Garner. His friend and student, Stirling Silliphant, was the screenwriter and had written the part specifically for Bruce. The movie version of *Marlowe* was based on Raymond Chandler's novel *The Little Sister*. Bruce, as diminutive, but sharply dressed Winslow Wong, stole the film in a scene where he destroyed Marlowe's office with his bare hands and feet! Bruce purchased the suits he wore in the film at Beverly Hills' Rodeo Drive boutiques, with the able assistance of close friend Ted Wong, who was on hand to offer moral support to Bruce for his first English-speaking Hollywood motion picture role.

1968, November 12 (Age 27)—Hollywood, Calif.: Bruce got more film work and was featured in an episode of *Blondie* entitled "Pick on a Bully Your Own Size," which featured Jim Backus (who played James Dean's father in *Rebel Without a Cause* and later provided the voice for the myopic "Mr. Magoo" cartoon character). Bruce also made other appearances in TV series; his agent procured him appearances on such television programs as *Hollywood Palace,* with Milton Berle.

1968, November 12-22 (Age 27)—Hollywood, Calif.: Bruce filmed his only adult non-martial-art role on the TV series *Here Come the Brides,* which featured a fresh-faced David Soul (Hutch of *Starsky & Hutch* fame) in an episode entitled "Marriage Chinese Style." He concluded this episode just five days before his 28th birthday.

1968, December (Age 28)—Culver City, Calif.: Bruce and his family had moved to a house on Van Buren Place in Culver City, a suburb of Los Angeles. This would prove to be only a temporary move, as Bruce's TV paychecks, plus residual fees for *The Green Hornet* reruns, led to Bruce and Linda scouting for a larger home. They moved to the upscale Bel Air location of 2551 Roscomare Road.

1969, January (Age 28)—Culver City, Calif.: With the help of Stirling Silliphant, Bruce began developing a movie script called *The Silent Flute.* A screenwriter, possibly Silliphant's nephew, was engaged for the initial treatment and was paid $12,000 by Stirling and James Coburn. However, the script written was deemed as unacceptable and no other scriptwriter seemed acceptable, so Bruce, Stirling, and James decided to collaborate and write it themselves. During this time, Stirling also helped support Bruce by helping to secure him other movie-related employment. In one such gesture, Silliphant hired Bruce as choreographer on a movie he'd scripted called *A Walk in the Spring Rain*.

1969, April 19 (Age 28)—Santa Monica, Calif.: Shortly after moving into the Bel Air home, Bruce and Linda's second child, Shannon Emery Lee, was born. Linda's maiden name served as Shannon's middle name. Bruce's reaction to his daughter's birth was, "An angel came to stay at our house."

1969, April 16-24 (Age 28)—Tennessee: Bruce traveled to Tennessee to choreograph the action scenes for the movie *A Walk in the Spring Rain*, starring Anthony Quinn and Ingrid Bergman. Pictures taken on the set show Bruce Lee, sharply attired in designer striped bell-bottoms, directing the action.

1969, May (Age 28)—Bel Air, Calif.: Robert Lee, Bruce Lee's younger brother, arrived from Hong Kong for a visit. Robert Lee had established himself as a pop rock singing star in Hong Kong. After seeing his younger brother at the airport and evaluating his slight physical frame, Bruce commented, "Don't tell anybody you're my brother; you'll embarrass me!"

1969, May 10-11 (Age 28)—Washington, D.C.: Bruce flew to Washington, D.C., as the special celebrity judge at Jhoon Rhee's 1969 National Karate Championships.

1969, June-July-August-September (Age 28)—Bel Air, Calif.: Bruce threw himself into his training with renewed exuberance. He also mounted a serious effort to train his celebrity clients, setting up a regular training regimen with his famous students in the back of his Bel Air home. Recently discovered home-movie footage of Bruce training his students during that time has emerged, showing scenes with celebrities James Coburn and Kareem Abdul-Jabbar, as well as showing Bruce training with Ted Wong, Dan Inosanto, Dan Lee, Herb Jackson, and numerous other JKD students from the Los Angeles area. It also shows Bruce kicking and punching a heavy bag at full speed and power and a young Brandon Bruce Lee doing his very best to constantly disrupt his father's training regime. Other footage has also been recently discovered from Australian producer Walt Missingham that shows Bruce Lee training actor James Coburn. This film, with a soundtrack dubbed by Bruce Lee himself, is called "the JKD tape." Some of this early footage was intended for Bruce's clients, to give them a way of seeing their "mistakes" in training. With it he could correct their form and technique and evaluate their improvement and overall performance.

1969, August 9 (Age 28)—Beverly Hills, Calif.: Bruce Lee's friend (and wife of his student, Roman Polanski) Sharon Tate was brutally murdered in her home at 10050 Cielo Drive in Beverly Hills, by the infamous Manson gang member, Linda Kasabian. Also murdered at Tate's home was Jay Sebring, the celebrity hairdresser whose influence with William Dozier led directly to Bruce Lee's first screen test in 1965. Sebring also helped to promote Bruce Lee among his own roster of celebrity clients, becoming an extremely influential part of Bruce Lee's rise to stardom. Bruce was naturally devastated at his inability to help save these murdered friends.

1970, February (Age 29)—Switzerland: Bruce flew to Switzerland to train his bereaved student, Roman Polanski, in gung-fu and to help ease the emotional stress caused by the recent murder of Roman's wife, Sharon Tate. On the way, Bruce stopped in London, England, to locate his stepbrother (who later became his right-hand man in Hong Kong), Wu Ngan. While in London, Bruce paid an exorbitant sum for a rare martial arts book. (Bruce was an avid collector of martial arts literature and during the course of his travels collected more than 2,000 books on all of the various fighting and pugilistic disciplines.)

1970, February (Age 29)—Dominican Republic: During Bruce's international travels, he visited the Dominican Republic to be a guest of Jhoon Rhee at a karate tournament taking place there.

1970, March (Age 29)—Hong Kong: Bruce, with his 5-year-old son Brandon, flew to Hong Kong to arrange a visa for his mother to move to the United States. As they left the plane, Bruce saw a huge contingent of the press surrounding the boarding ramp. He looked around to see what celebrity had been on board, and was astonished to discover that the fuss was over him. His role as Kato in *The Green Hornet*, which was being syndicated in Hong Kong as *The Kato Show*, had made him very popular. Bruce was immediately booked on a Hong Kong television show where both he and his son Brandon gave an impromptu demonstration of board-breaking; they were quite simply a sensation. Bruce had suddenly discovered that he was a true star in the Asian media markets.

Also during his visit in Hong Kong, Bruce developed the idea and a business plan for a possible movie deal. He sent his friend and fellow Hong Kong actor Unicorn Chan (who portrayed Siu Kay Lun, a popular James Bond-like character, in several films and who later died in a car accident) to present the idea to Run Run Shaw on his behalf and to inform Shaw that Bruce would be willing to do a movie for him for US$10,000. Shaw made a counteroffer of a seven-year contract and US$2,000 per film, which Bruce declined.

1970, May 24 (Age 29)—Washington, D.C.: Bruce once again appeared as a celebrity guest at Jhoon Rhee's National Karate Championships, held in Washington, D.C. His popularity was as big as ever and he visited a number of friends and martial artists whom he hadn't seen in a while.

1970, June (Age 29)—Hollywood, Calif.: Bruce had several lengthy meetings and began serious negotiations with James Coburn and Warner Bros. to secure backing for *The Silent Flute* project, which he, James Coburn, and screenwriter Stirling Silliphant had been developing.

1970, August (Age 29)—Los Angeles, Calif.: While training, Bruce injured his sacral nerve and experienced severe muscle spasms in his lower back. He had been performing a strenuous weight exercise, which involved nearly 100 pounds of weight on a bar across his neck. The doctors told him that he would never be able to kick again and would possibly even need to give up martial arts. This bad news only gave Bruce more incentive to fight the diagnosis; he was determined to regain his fitness. While bedridden and during the months of his recovery, he began to document his training methods and his philosophy of jeet kune do. He made many notes documenting fight strategies, drew explicit "technique" figures, quoted philosophical sayings that pertained to the martial arts, and established highly precise text notations about the many aspects of The Way of the Intercepting Fist. (After his death, *The Tao of Jeet Kune Do* was published by his wife in his memory.)

Although Bruce did recover more fully from his injury than the doctors had predicted, he would never completely regain full mobility in his back and would continue to take cortisone painkillers for the rest of his life.

1970, October 19 (Age 29)—Hollywood, Calif.: Bruce got word from Stirling Silliphant that the final draft for *The Silent Flute* was finished. Though still somewhat incapacitated by his injury, Bruce was elated to learn that the renowned martial arts publication *Black Belt* magazine would be featuring an article titled "The Making of *The Silent Flute*."

1970, December (Age 30)—Los Angeles, Calif.: To help supplement their diminished income, Linda Lee took a position working for a telephone answering service. Bruce was severely embarrassed and somewhat distraught, but he did the necessary task of babysitting 5-year-old Brandon and eighteen-month-old Shannon. He also was being referred from doctor to doctor for back treatment. Using nothing more than a combination of mind over matter, painkillers, and his incredible will to succeed, Bruce continued to push forward with his projects.

1971, February (Age 30)—India: Bruce, James Coburn, and Stirling Silliphant flew to India to scout locations for *The Silent Flute*. They spent one month looking but were forced to call off the search when Coburn backed out of the project, taking Warner Bros.' financing with him. After all the previous planning and the work on the script, Bruce was distraught because it left him with no future job prospects in sight. The only consolation was that the trip to India gave Bruce the idea for *Game of Death*, a movie about a fighter who is a master in several techniques and who, entering a temple, must fight his way from one level to the next. Each level would involve a different aspect; the first level would be the level of weaponry, the second the level of the 9th degree black belt, and the third the level of the unknown.

1971, May (Age 30)—Hollywood, Calif.: Bruce had talks with Warner Bros. executives, including Fred Weintraub and Jerry Leider, for a TV series based on a Chinese Shaolin monk and set in the Old West during the 1800s. This series was tentatively titled *The Warrior.* Bruce quickly helped to develop a project he felt would empower him on U.S. TV screens.

1971, June 15 (Age 30)—Bel Air, Calif.: Bruce was called at 4 a.m. by a Hong Kong radio announcer and interviewed live on the air. Bruce was asked many questions about his plans and television career. One of the questions asked was whether he planned to make any films in Hong Kong. In response to the disc jockey's question, Bruce jokingly replied he would make a movie in Asia "if the price was right." This interview was heard by Golden Harvest executive Raymond Chow, who dispatched one of his producers, Mrs. Lo Wei, to offer Bruce a contract. Bruce was unsure about accepting because he was in the process of developing *The Warrior* script for TV. He consulted several friends about doing movies in foreign countries; James Coburn advised him by simply saying, "TV wastes genius... follow Eastwood and Bronson; make a movie abroad."

1971, June 24 to July 1 (Age 30)—Hollywood, Calif.: Bruce's television career began to gain momentum, yet he yearned to be featured on the big screen. He was receiving critical acclaim for his appearances and acting talents on television. His portrayal of Li Tsung in the pilot episode of TV's *Longstreet* was lauded as his finest screen appearance.

1971, June 28 (Age 30)—Bel Air, Calif.: After discussing the fine points of the Golden Harvest contract with Lo Wei, Bruce decided to follow his friend James Coburn's advice and took advantage of the international opportunity by signing to a two-picture deal.

1971, July 23 (Age 30)—Thailand: Bruce Lee flew to Thailand to make his first Chinese movie as an adult, *The Big Boss*. Bruce was supplied with a small furnished apartment at 2 Man Wan Road in Kowloon, Hong Kong. His stepbrother, Wu Ngan, moved in with Bruce and Linda and when Wu Ngan later married, his new wife moved in as well.

In the movie, Bruce plays Chen, a young man sent to live with relatives and to work with them in a local ice factory. Chen stumbles upon a cache of drugs hidden in the ice and his family is murdered in revenge. The film's finale shows Bruce Lee defeating the gangsters with a fighting passion seldom seen before or since.

1971, September 3 (Age 30)—Hong Kong: Bruce returned to Hong Kong from Thailand to host a press conference at Kai Tak airport. Because Bruce was established as a television star in the United States, the press was anxious to learn more about his future plans since he had become one of the very first ethnic Chinese to gain worldwide acceptance in the entertainment industry. The people of Hong Kong were excited that Bruce had become so well recognized.

1971, September 4 (Age 30)—Hong Kong: Having obtained the necessary visa, Bruce took several days to arrange for his mother, Grace Lee, to move to the U.S.

Bruce was interviewed by Canadian talk show host, Pierre Berton, for a TV program being filmed in Hong Kong. (This is the only filmed interview said to be in existence.)

Brandon attended La Salle College, which was the same school Bruce attended only 15 years before.

1971, September 16 (Age 30)—United States: The pilot episode of *Longstreet* aired and Bruce received more fan mail than lead actor James Franciscus. The episode was titled "The Way of the Intercepting Fist," which was the literal translation for Bruce Lee's jeet kune do. The episode was, in fact, the result of a close collaboration between Silliphant and Bruce; both worked on the script. Franciscus portrayed a blind detective who is taught martial arts by Bruce's character, Li Tsung. This episode showcased Bruce Lee's philosophy perfectly, and Bruce received rave reviews in the *New York Times*. (Bruce would later appear in three more episodes, "Spell Legacy Like Death," "I See, Said the Blind Man," and "Wednesday's Child.")

1971, September (Age 30)—United States: Bruce Lee is featured on the cover of *Black Belt* magazine. The feature article entitled "Liberate Yourself from Classical Karate" would be the last one personally submitted by Bruce and was a gracious gesture to his friend, mentor, and *Black Belt* publisher, Mito Uyehara. Mito, like Silliphant, had championed Bruce at every opportunity, with mutually beneficial results as it also increased the sales of his martial arts magazine. The article was an early example of Bruce's retelling of the Zen concept "the usefulness of a cup is in its emptiness." He finished his article by stating that his thoughts were merely "a finger pointing to the moon," a concept he later re-emphasized in *Enter the Dragon* to great effect. To further emphasize his point, Bruce had his friend George Lee create a tombstone that read "In memory of a once fluid man crammed and distorted by the classical mess." A picture of the tombstone was published with the article and created quite a bit of controversy in the martial arts community.

1971, October (Age 30)—Hong Kong: Bruce returned to Hong Kong with his wife Linda and his two children for *The Big Boss* premiere, staying in the temporary apartment at 2 Man Wan Road, Waterloo Hill. The city was in an uproar over the movie; *The Big Boss* opened to great reviews and mobs of fans and grossed more than 3.5 million Hong Kong dollars in just nineteen days, outstripping previous record holder *The Sound of Music* by more than $1 million. It would later be released in the U.S. as *Fists of Fury*. Bruce Lee's life would never return to normal; he was mobbed in Hong Kong wherever he went. Bruce, who was accompanied by his Oakland student Robert (Bob) Baker (acting as his bodyguard), appeared with Baker on Hong Kong TV to promote the release of *The Big Boss*. Following the press previews, local English journalist Ted Thomas interviewed Bruce for Hong Kong radio for what was to be his last radio interview. Because of this, the interview is often referred to as "the last interview."

1971, December 7 (Age 31)—Hong Kong: Bruce received a telegram from Warner Bros. executive Jerry Leider, notifying him that he had not been chosen for the part in the upcoming series *The Warrior*. (The series was later released as *Kung-Fu* and starred non-martial-artist David Carradine. It first aired as ABC-TV's Movie of the Week on February 21, 1972.)

1971, December 9 (Age 31)—Hong Kong: Bruce's only released English-language interview airs, having been filmed in September 1971 with Canadian broadcaster Pierre Berton. (This interview is often referred to as the "lost interview," as it disappeared for several years until it was eventually found in a storage facility.)

1971, December (Age 31)—Bel Air, Calif.: Following the disappointing news from Warner Bros. about not being given the lead role in

The Warrior, Bruce and Linda sold their home in Bel Air, California, and permanently relocated the family to Hong Kong. This move also enabled him to begin work on his second movie for Golden Harvest, *The Chinese Connection.* Bruce got a larger budget and salary, and more power in the directing of this film, and it was the first one to feature his "signature" fighting style—using strange cries and the nunchaku (rice flail) weapon. Robert Baker, a former student of Bruce and James Yimm Lee from Oakland, California, appeared as the Russian villain in the movie. Bob also acted as Bruce Lee's personal bodyguard during filming to allow Bruce the privacy he required from overly ardent admirers.

The story, based on fact, is set in Shanghai at the turn of the century. Bruce's character, once again named Chen, is the top Chinese boxer of the Ching-Wu school. A local Japanese karate school terrorizes Chen's colleagues and murders his Sifu (teacher), requiring Chen to exact a bloodthirsty and exciting revenge.

1972, January (Age 31)—Hong Kong: Bruce Lee's third Golden Harvest movie was to be another period drama, directed by Lo Wei (who had also directed the first two). However, Bruce, being dissatisfied with Lo's inattention to detail, declined the film. Instead, he elected to develop, write, direct, and star in his own production, *The Dragon Has Entered* (the title was later changed to *Way of the Dragon*).

1972, February (Age 31)—United States: The first episode of the *Kung-Fu* TV series (originally named *The Warrior*) aired in the United States.

1972, March (Age 31)—Hong Kong: *The Chinese Connection* was released. It grossed even more than *The Big Boss* and further established Bruce as a Hong Kong superstar. Bruce Lee became a partner with Raymond Chow, forming their own production company, Concord Pictures.

1972, April (Age 31)—Hong Kong: Bruce's film salaries and earnings had enabled him and Linda to re-establish more permanency in their lifestyle. He used a portion of the proceeds from his first two very successful movies and paid more than $1 million Hong Kong dollars for a palatial detached mansion at 41 Cumberland Road in Kowloon. From here, he began earnestly developing his first project as a director of a major motion picture, *Way of the Dragon*.

1972, May 1 (Age 31)—Hong Kong: Golden Harvest held a farewell party for the *Way of the Dragon* film crew that Bruce was sending to Rome, Italy, one of the primary locations for the movie.

1972, May 4 (Age 31)—Rome, Italy: Bruce Lee, Raymond Chow, and a Japanese cameraman flew to Rome, Italy. There they were met by *Way of the Dragon* co-stars Bob Wall and U.S. karate champion Chuck Norris. For this film production, which he wrote, directed, and starred in, Bruce received almost complete control. Chuck Norris is Bruce's adversary in the final fight scene. This film would later surpass all records set by his previous two films.

1972, May (Age 31)—Hong Kong: Bruce began work on *Game of Death* and filmed several fight scenes with Danny Inosanto and Kareem Abdul-Jabbar.

Bruce appeared on Hong Kong's TV B channel for a hurricane disaster relief benefit. As a demonstration, Bruce broke four out of five boards, one of which was hanging in the air on a line of string. His 7-year-old son Brandon even performed and broke a board with a side-kick!

Bruce helped Unicorn Chan, a fellow actor, by assisting him for one day and supervising some fight action sequences in Unicorn's film, *The Unicorn Palm* (also known as *Fist of Unicorn*). Footage of Bruce on the set was used in the movie, and Bruce's name appeared in the credits, to his surprise. Bruce became angry and made a public announcement denying his endorsement of the film. Unicorn had been advised to put Bruce's name in the credits to provide his movie with a better chance of success.

1972, October (Age 31)—Hollywood, Calif.: Ted Ashley, a Warner Bros. executive, offers Bruce and Raymond Chow the chance to work with noted film producers Fred Weintraub and Paul Heller on the first-ever film project collaboration between Hollywood and Hong Kong. Seeing an excellent opportunity, Bruce immediately seized it and flew to the United States to finalize the project, secure his role, and sign the necessary motion picture contracts. The film would eventually be released as *Enter the Dragon.*

1972, December 28 (Age 32)—Oakland, Calif.: Bruce's martial arts brother, confidant, and close friend, James Yimm Lee, died of "black lung" (cancer) in Oakland, California, at the age of 52. Bruce, having received the news by telephone and later by letter, was greatly bereaved at the loss.

1973, January (Age 32)—Hong Kong: The *Enter the Dragon* production company from the United States arrived in Hong Kong under the directorship of Robert Clouse and principle development began. Co-star John Saxon had already filmed his golf scenes in Los Angeles, California, in late 1972.

1973, February 8 (Age 32)—Hong Kong: Bruce paid a return visit to his Hong Kong school La Salle College for an award ceremony.

1973, February (Age 32)—Hong Kong: Bruce put *Game of Death* production on hold when principle filming of *Enter the Dragon* began in Hong Kong. It was the first combined production of the U.S. and Hong Kong film industries and was co-produced by the Sequoia, Concord, and Warner Bros. production companies.

The film centers around "Lee" (played by Bruce Lee), a Shaolin monk who is invited to attend a martial arts tournament on a remote island in the China Sea owned by the renegade monk Han (played by veteran Hong Kong actor Shek Kin). Han uses the tournament to recruit dubious characters for his opium smuggling operation.

Enter the Dragon featured American star John Saxon, fresh from his role opposite Clint Eastwood in *Joe Kidd*; U.S. karate champion Bob Wall, who had appeared in *Way of the Dragon*, as the villain "O'Hara"; and Jim Kelly, who would go on to appear in several kung-fu/karate black-exploitation movies like *Black Belt Jones*, as "Williams." Angela Mao Ying played Lee's sister; English character actor Geoffrey Weeks appeared as Braithwaite (the representative of interested governments); and Australian Peter Archer, who ran a Hong Kong karate dojo at the time, appeared in a cameo role at Bruce's invitation. Also featured was Sammo Hung, now a renowned director in Hong Kong, as the Shaolin monk whom Lee defeats in the opening segment of the movie. Appearing in a stunt role was a young Jackie Chan; in the stunt, his neck is broken by Lee during a fight in the cave. (Jackie had also doubled the role of Suzuki in *The Chinese Connection*, having been kicked backward through a screen door during the final sequence.) Tony Liu, a close friend of Bruce Lee, also had a small role and was the only actor to appear in all of Bruce's completed movies in the 1970s.

1973, February 20 (Age 32)—Hong Kong: Bruce was the guest of honor at St. Francis Xavier College for Sports Day ceremonies.

1973, March (Age 32)—Hong Kong: Principle filming for *Enter the Dragon* was completed.

1973, April (Age 32)—Hong Kong: American actor James Coburn, Bruce's friend and student, visited Hong Kong to persuade Bruce to resume *The Silent Flute* project. He and Bruce gave an impromptu photo opportunity for the press at Kai Tak airport. (Stirling Silliphant would later undertake a similar mission, but both Silliphant and Coburn met with little success.) *The Silent Flute* was eventually made into the movie *Circle of Iron,* starring David Carradine, in 1978.

1973, April (Age 32)—Hong Kong: Filming of *Enter the Dragon* was completed.

1973, May 10 (Age 32)—Hong Kong: Bruce was at Golden Harvest Studios in Hong Kong dubbing his voice and adding the sound effects for the *Enter the Dragon* fight sequences. The air conditioners had been turned off so the microphones would not pick up their sound, and the temperature and humidity in the isolated dubbing rooms were very high. Taking a break to go to the bathroom and splash water on his face, Bruce passed out on the bathroom floor. Twenty minutes later, an assistant sent to find him discovered him just as Bruce began reviving. He tried to conceal his collapse by acting as though he had dropped his glasses, but he collapsed again on the way back to the dubbing room and began convulsing. Bruce was rushed to nearby Baptist Hospital, where he was examined by neurosurgeons Dr. Thomas Langford and Dr. Peter Woo.

Bruce Lee had experienced muscle contractions and his breathing was abnormal; he was given mannitol to reduce an apparent but unaccountable swelling of his brain. After only about five hours, a dramatic change in his condition occurred. He could smile to his wife Linda, but his speech came slowly and was slurred. His blood tests showed a possible kidney malfunction. Bruce recovered after twenty-four hours, stating he had "felt near death…" but had refused to give up, fearing that if he had he would have died.

1973, May 25 (Age 32)—Los Angeles, Calif.: Bruce flew to the United States for a series of exploratory tests at the Los Angeles Medical Center, performed by Dr. Harold Karpman and Dr. David Reisbord. A brain scan and brain-flow study were performed, as well as a complete physical and EEG. The tests detected no brain abnormalities, although the doctors were certain that Bruce had suffered a "cerebral edema," or swelling of the fluid surrounding the brain, as well as a type of convulsion called a "grand mal idiopathic," although they could find no known cause for either. To help prevent reoccurrence and to control this malady, Bruce was prescribed Dilantin.

While in California, Bruce visited with Dan Inosanto, and his mother (who had relocated to the United States). During his visit with his mother, he prophetically remarked to her that he felt he did not have long to live and told her not to worry about finances as he would make sure she was provided for. She rebuked him for talking in such a way.

He also visited the Warner Bros. lot to view a rough-cut print of *Enter the Dragon.* This contained editor's crayon marks with no music effects, but was mainly a finished edit. Bruce was, by all accounts, delighted with the results and felt he'd done a fine job of acting in the film. Deep inside he also knew that this was going to be a blockbuster that would bring him worldwide fame. (It must be stated that most of the effective scenes from *Enter the Dragon* were purely Bruce Lee's own ideas, such as the opening fight in the temple, which he had convinced the producers to add to help introduce the "Lee" character. Ironically, this was also the final fight scene that Bruce Lee would ever shoot. It featured Sammo Hung as his rotund, acrobatic opponent.)

1973, July 10 (Age 32)—Hong Kong: While walking through the Golden Harvest Studios, Bruce overheard director Lo Wei boasting loudly that Bruce Lee's success was entirely due to his (Lo Wei's) directing abilities. Bruce entered the office and began arguing with the old man and his wife, Mrs. Lo Wei (who had signed Bruce Lee for *The Big Boss* role). When Lo Wei stormed off, Bruce followed and confronted him. Lo Wei summoned the local police and on their arrival, falsely accused Bruce of threatening him with a knife he had concealed in his belt buckle. Bruce, unwisely, retorted that if he had wanted to kill Lo Wei he'd have used only two fingers, not a knife. This led to further ugly scenes, with the result that Bruce, in an effort to quell further arguments, agreed to sign a paper promising to leave Lo Wei in peace. Lo Wei further insisted that Bruce sign a statement that he would not harm Lo Wei; though his having threatened Lo Wei with a knife was a complete fabrication, Bruce reluctantly signed the statement simply to pacify Lo Wei.

Later that same day, Bruce appeared on the Hong Kong TV show, *Enjoy Yourself Tonight,* with host Ho Sho Shin. Bruce alluded to his problems with director Lo Wei, but did not mention him by name. Bruce was asked to demonstrate his abilities, using the TV host as an opponent. When the demonstration resulted in Shin being hurled across the stage, it appeared that the host believed that Bruce had struck a little harder than necessary. This overzealous display of power would lead to accusations from the press that Bruce was becoming egotistical about his status as a film star, and he was virtually indicted in the newspapers of bullying the talk show host (though this was not the case). Though Bruce attempted to put the record straight on HKTV-B, his every word, deed, and move were being viewed in a negative light. This fresh controversy found a home in some of the tabloids that earned money from sensationalism, and Bruce soon became a "gossip item" in every tabloid in Southeast Asia.

1973, July 16 (Age 32)—Hong Kong: During a $200 telephone call to Bruce's friend and fellow actor, Unicorn Chan, who was filming a movie in Manila, the Philippines, Bruce revealed he was worried about the many headaches he had been experiencing.

1973, July 18 (Age 32)—Hong Kong: A *feng shui* deflector on the roof of Bruce's Cumberland Road home in Hong Kong was blown off by heavy rain and winds. The deflector had been placed to protect Bruce and his family from bad feng shui by warding off evil spirits. The previous owners had been plagued by financial disaster and the cause was believed to be due to the incorrect positioning of the house.

1973, July 20 (Age 32)—Hong Kong: Early in the morning, Bruce typed a letter to his attorney Adrian Marshall, detailing business ventures he wished to discuss during his upcoming publicity tour to Los Angeles, California. Bruce had already purchased tickets for his trip and was scheduled to appear on the Johnny Carson show.

Raymond Chow came by to discuss plans for their upcoming movie, *Game of Death,* and took Bruce to visit Betty Ting Pei at her apartment to discuss her role in the film. Plans for later that evening included a meeting with actor George Lazenby over dinner to enlist him for a part. While at Betty's, Bruce, complaining of a headache, took a prescription painkiller of Betty's and lay down on her bed to rest prior to dinner. Raymond departed, intending to meet them later at the restaurant. At 9 p.m., while Raymond and George

Lazenby waited for Bruce and Betty at the restaurant, Raymond received a frantic call from Betty; she had been unable to awaken Bruce. At Raymond's suggestion, she summoned her personal physician, who, also unable to revive Bruce, had him taken to the hospital. After further efforts to revive him, Bruce was pronounced dead. The doctors at the hospital were surprised that he had lasted as long as he had that night, but unfortunately Betty had not gotten him help immediately.

Bruce Lee died of an apparent cerebral edema (swelling of the brain) and after much confusion and debate, doctors declared his death to be a "death by misadventure." (During the inquest, it would later transpire that Bruce Lee had "probably" suffered an allergic reaction to Meprobamate, an ingredient in the tablets that Betty Ting Pei had given him.)

The premiere of *Enter the Dragon* was delayed by four days because of the actor's death.

1973, July 25—Hong Kong: A funeral ceremony was held for friends and fans in Hong Kong, consisting of more than 25,000 people. Bruce was dressed in the Chinese outfit he wore in *Enter the Dragon*.

1973, July 30—Seattle, Wash.: After a smaller second ceremony in Seattle, Washington, at Butterworth Funeral Home on East Pine Street, Bruce Lee was buried at Lake View Cemetery. His pallbearers included Steve McQueen, James Coburn, Danny Inosanto, Taky Kimura, Peter Chin, and his brother, Robert Lee.

1973, August 24—Hollywood, Calif.: *Enter the Dragon* premieres at Grauman's Chinese Theatre. The movie is a success, and Bruce Lee achieves worldwide fame.

Appendix

Officially Certifiable Original Oakland JKD Students

Bob Baker

Ernie Benevidez

Gary Cagaanan

Richard Carney

Harry Chin

Bill Christensen

David Cox

Joseph "Joe" Davis

Tom And Jan De Laurel

Gary Dill

Leo Fong

Mike Fong

Dr. Lloyd Freitas

Robert Garcia

Rodney Gee

Barry Hay

Gary Hum

Allen Joe

Jerome Lai

Eric Lee

George Lee

Greglon Yimm Lee

Russell Lee

Moon Ling

Felix Macias, Sr.

Allen And Mario Magdangal

Hank Maguire

Bob Marshall

Fred Meredith

Al Novak

Jimmy Ong

Stan Piasik

Manuel Rodriquez

Gordon Toy

Howard Williams

Alvin Wong

Dr. Arnold Wong

Curtis Yee

Ed Kim Yee

Edward Yee

David Young

Acknowledgments

James Yimm Lee Memorabilia
Greglon Yimm Lee

Bruce Lee Photographs
Bruce Lee Educational Foundation

Digital Transcription
Bruce Faron
Sid Campbell

North Atlantic Books, Frog, Ltd.,
Project Editor: Anastasia McGhee
Book Design: Brad Greene
Editing: Robin Klassen
Jude Anthony
Richard Baca
Michael Bishop
Annie Shear
Sid Campbell
Adrienne Armstrong

Negative Scanning
Martin Eng

Photo Contributions
Karena Lee *(Oakland Chronicle)*

Bruce Lee's Obituary
The New York Times

James Yimm Lee's Obituary
The Oakland Tribune

Marketing-Publicity
Robert Alsted

Letter Contributors

Al Novak

George Lee

Bob Baker

Allen Joe

Felix Macias, Sr.

Jasper Cummings

Ed Kim Yee

George Tom

Leo Fong

Gary Cagaanan

Jim Wong

Robert Garcia, Jr.

Ernest Benevidez

Hilton Wong

Wally Jay

Ed Parker

Ralph Castro

Dan Inosanto

Sam Allred

Jon Lee

Karena Beverly Lee

Greglon Yimm Lee

Bryant Wong

Ricky Ramirez

Aloy and Claire Brunk

Dr. James Durkins

Dr. Lloyd A. Freitas

Ming Lum

Dr. Norman Marks

Sid Campbell

Eric Lee

Howard Williams

Al Dacascos

Hank Maguire

Joseph "Joe" Davis

Richard Siu

About the Authors

Sid Campbell and Greglon Yimm Lee are the authors of *The Dragon and the Tiger: The Birth of Bruce Lee's Jeet Kune Do, The Oakland Years: Volume 1* (Frog, Ltd., 2003) and *The Dragon and the Tiger: The Untold Story of Jun Fan Gung-fu and James Yimm Lee, The Oakland Years: Volume 2* (Frog, Ltd., 2005).

A leading authority on traditional Okinawan and Japanese martial arts, SID CAMPBELL holds a 10th degree black belt (Hanshi-grandmaster) in shorin-ryu karate and currently supervises more than 48 shorin-ryu branch schools around the world.

Campbell has produced major martial arts tournaments and expositions, appeared in numerous motion pictures, been featured in instructional video programs, awarded more than 850 black belts, and taught more than 15,000 students. He is an artist, lecturer, inventor, scriptwriter, and World Martial Art Masters Association Hall of Fame inductee, as well as a featured founding member of www.worldblackbelt.com. Campbell has written more than 50 books related to his career as a martial arts teacher and educator including *Ninja Shuriken Throwing, Balisong: Lethal Filipino Knife Fighting, Renzokuken: Toudi-jutsu's Awesome Continuous Fist Fighting Strategies, Weapons of the Samurai: Bushido Arts of War,* and *The Shorin-ryu Encyclopedia.* He had the opportunity to share martial arts knowledge with both Bruce Lee and James Yimm Lee when they visited his dojo in Oakland, California, during the late 1960s.

Visit Sid Campbell's websites at
www.Oaklandjkd.com and www.Sidcampbell.net.

GREGLON YIMM LEE is a practitioner of jeet kune do, a promoter of civic functions, and a co-producer of martial arts instructional videotapes. Lee's involvement with the study of martial arts has prompted him to carry on the jeet kune do concepts that were developed by his father, James Yimm Lee, and Bruce Lee. He has been teaching these concepts for more than twenty years. In addition, Greglon Lee is actively engaged in reprinting many of the original books and literary works published by his father. These include *Modern Kung-Fu Karate: Iron and Poison Hand Training* and *Fighting Arts of the Orient: Elemental Karate and Kung-Fu,* as well as others that were previously unpublished.

Check out the Official Dragon and Tiger Website
<http://www.Oaklandjkd.com/> now online!